Elixir & Phoei
Modern Applications

A practical guide to Mastering Your Web Development Skills with Elixir and Phoenix Frameworks

Jose Krum

Table of Contents

Preface   **4**

Chapter 1: Why Elixir and Phoenix?   **7**

   1.1: The Evolving Web Development Landscape   7

   1.2: Introducing Elixir: Your Functional Programming Powerhouse   11

   1.3: Phoenix Framework: Built for Speed and Scalability   13

Chapter 2: Mastering Elixir Fundamentals   **17**

   2.1: Syntax and Data Structures   17

   2.2: Functional Programming: Thinking in Pure Functions   21

   2.3: Pattern Matching: Elegance and Efficiency   24

Chapter 3: Unveiling Phoenix Framework   **29**

   3.1: Architecture and the MVC Pattern   29

   3.2: Controllers and Actions: Handling User Requests   34

   3.3: Views and Templates: Presenting Data Beautifully   37

Chapter 4: Data Management with Ecto   **46**

   4.1: Connecting to Databases and Schemas   46

   4.2: CRUD Operations: The Life Cycle of Your Data   51

   4.3: Advanced Queries and Relationships   57

Chapter 5: Secure Your App: Authentication and Authorization   **64**

   5.2: Authorization Best Practices with Plug   71

   5.3: Implementing Role-Based Access Control   81

Chapter 6: Real-time Interactions with Phoenix Channels   **94**

   6.1: Introduction to WebSockets and Channels   94

   6.2: Building Chat Applications and Live Feeds   96

   6.3: Broadcasting Updates and Real-time Collaboration   104

Chapter 7: APIs and Beyond: RESTful & GraphQL   **112**

   7.1: Building RESTful APIs   112

   7.2: Integrating GraphQL for Flexible Data Access   118

   7.3: Exploring Other API Strategies   124

Chapter 8: Unlocking Performance: Concurrency and Optimization 129

   8.1: Elixir's Concurrency Model - Processes and GenServers   129

   8.2: Optimizing Application Performance for Scalability   136

8.3: Monitoring and Debugging Techniques   142

Chapter 9: Building Scalable and Distributed Systems   **148**

9.1: Introduction to Distributed Systems with Elixir   148

9.2: Cluster Management and Supervision Trees   151

9.3: Fault Tolerance and High Availability Strategies   157

Chapter 10: Advanced Phoenix Features and Security   **162**

10.1 Hot Reloading and Code Generation for Efficiency   162

10.2 Testing Strategies: Unit and Integration Testing   168

10.3: Security Best Practices and Common Vulnerabilities   174

Bonus Chapter: Real-world Case Studies and Applications   **181**

Conclusion   **184**

Preface

Are you ready to ditch the tired, old frameworks and embrace a new level of power, clarity, and fun in your coding journey? Look no further than Elixir and Phoenix, a dynamic duo poised to revolutionize your development experience.

We've all been there – the frustration of wrestling with complex frameworks, battling concurrency issues, and yearning for code that's not just functional, but beautiful. That's where Elixir and Phoenix step in, offering a breath of fresh air. Elixir, with its elegant syntax and functional programming approach, makes crafting clean, maintainable code a breeze. Phoenix, built on top of Elixir, provides a robust yet flexible structure for building lightning-fast, scalable web applications.

This book is your one-stop shop for mastering this dynamic duo. Whether you're a seasoned developer looking to expand your toolkit or a curious beginner eager to explore new horizons, we've got you covered. We'll guide you through the fundamentals of Elixir, unravel the secrets of Phoenix, and equip you with the skills to build modern, cutting-edge web applications.

We've structured this book to be an intuitive and engaging journey. We'll start with the core building blocks of Elixir, guiding you through its syntax, data structures, and functional programming concepts. Then, we'll dive into the heart of Phoenix, showcasing its architecture, controllers, views, and routing. From there, we'll delve into real-world application development, covering everything from data management with Ecto to building APIs and real-time experiences with WebSockets. Finally, we'll equip you with advanced techniques for optimizing performance, building scalable systems, and ensuring the security of your applications.

So, are you ready to embark on this exciting adventure? Buckle up, open your coding editor, and prepare to be amazed by the power and elegance of Elixir and Phoenix. This book is not just a technical guide, it's a gateway to a new way of thinking, coding, and building web applications. With each chapter, you'll discover the joy of writing clean, concise, and maintainable code, while simultaneously creating applications that are fast, scalable, and truly enjoyable to build. Let's get started!

Chapter 1: Why Elixir and Phoenix?

Think of the current web development landscape as a crowded highway. Everyone's trying to get to the same destination (amazing web applications), but the traffic's a nightmare, the lanes are confusing, and the cars are all sputtering along on outdated engines. That's where Elixir and Phoenix come in, offering a sleek, high-performance sports car to cruise past the gridlock and reach your destination in style.

1.1: The Evolving Web Development Landscape

Just like electric cars revolutionized transportation, new tools are emerging to transform web development. This section is your roadmap, highlighting why the current landscape needs a change and how Elixir and Phoenix offer a refreshing alternative.

The Bottlenecks of Traditional Frameworks:

Imagine building a website with a framework that feels like a gas-guzzling SUV. Sure, it might get you there, but at what cost? Here are some common pain points:

- Scalability struggles: As your user base grows, the framework starts chugging, unable to handle the increased traffic. It's like trying to tow a trailer with a compact car – slow and inefficient.
- Concurrency woes: Handling multiple requests simultaneously becomes a juggling act, leading to errors and performance issues. Think rush hour traffic – everyone's trying to move at once, and chaos ensues.
- Code complexity: The framework itself might be bulky and convoluted, making your code harder to read, maintain, and debug. It's like deciphering a tangled mess of wires under the hood – frustrating and time-consuming.

These challenges aren't just theoretical; they can seriously impact your development experience and the quality of your applications. The good news is, there's a growing demand for better tools, and that's where Elixir and Phoenix come in.

The Rise of Functional Programming and Scalability:

Think of Elixir and Phoenix as sleek, high-performance electric vehicles built for the modern web development highway. They address the key issues mentioned earlier with a powerful combination of:

- Functional programming: This paradigm emphasizes immutability (data doesn't change), pure functions (predictable outcomes), and pattern matching (elegant data manipulation). It's like writing clean, modular code that's easy to understand and maintain – think organized tool boxes with everything in its place.
- Concurrency built-in: Elixir's Erlang Virtual Machine (BEAM) excels at handling multiple tasks simultaneously, ensuring your application stays responsive even under heavy load. Imagine multiple lanes of traffic flowing smoothly, each car reaching its destination efficiently.
- Lightweight and scalable: Both Elixir and Phoenix are designed to be lean and mean, using resources efficiently and scaling effortlessly as your application grows. It's like a car that gets amazing mileage and effortlessly adapts to different terrains.

But wait, there's more! Elixir and Phoenix also offer a plethora of features that streamline development and create amazing user experiences. We'll explore these in detail throughout the book, but for now, remember this:

- Hot reloading: Changes in your code reflect instantly, saving you time and frustration. It's like having a mechanic who instantly fixes your car without needing to restart the engine.

- WebSockets: Real-time communication enables dynamic features like chat applications and live dashboards. Imagine your car having built-in walkie-talkies, keeping you connected to your users in real-time.
- Powerful tooling: Built-in features like Ecto for database interactions and Absinthe for GraphQL integration make complex tasks a breeze. Think of it as having a set of specialized tools that makes every repair or upgrade on your car easier and faster.

The web development landscape is evolving, and the tools you choose matter. If you're tired of the limitations of traditional frameworks and yearn for a more efficient, enjoyable development experience, then Elixir and Phoenix are worth exploring. This book will be your guide, equipping you with the knowledge and skills to navigate the open road of modern web development. Buckle up, and let's get started!

Remember, the journey doesn't stop here. Stay tuned for the next section, where we'll dive deeper into the world of Elixir and unlock its functional programming magic!

1.2: Introducing Elixir: Your Functional Programming Powerhouse

Elixir is a dynamically typed language built on top of the Erlang Virtual Machine (BEAM). This might sound technical, but here's the cool part: BEAM is renowned for its fault tolerance and concurrency handling. Think of it as a powerful engine that can handle multiple tasks simultaneously, even under pressure. It's ideal for building applications that need to be always on and responsive, like chat platforms or e-commerce websites.

But Elixir isn't just about speed and efficiency. It embraces functional programming: a paradigm that emphasizes writing clean, concise, and easy-to-understand code. Imagine building your machine with modular components that fit together perfectly, reducing complexity and making debugging a breeze. Here are some key principles of functional programming that Elixir champions:

- Immutability: Data doesn't change once it's created, leading to fewer bugs and easier reasoning about your code. Think of each component in your machine having a fixed purpose and function, making the overall system predictable and reliable.

- Pure functions: Functions always produce the same output for the same input, making them predictable and easily testable. Imagine each tool in your toolbox always performing the same task flawlessly, giving you consistent results every time.
- Pattern matching: This powerful technique lets you extract and manipulate data in elegant ways. Think of it as having a Swiss Army knife that can handle various tasks efficiently and intuitively.

Learning Elixir: A Step-by-Step Approach

Don't worry; we'll unpack these concepts gradually throughout the book. We'll start with the basics, like syntax and data structures, and build your understanding step-by-step. Think of it as assembling your toolbox piece by piece, learning the function of each tool and how they work together.

Here are some practical benefits of using Elixir:

- Reduced complexity: Functional programming promotes cleaner code, making your applications easier to maintain and understand. Imagine a well-organized toolbox where everything has its place, saving you time and frustration when you need a specific tool.
- Fewer bugs: Immutability and pure functions help prevent errors, leading to more reliable and

stable applications. Think of your machine running smoothly without unexpected breakdowns, ensuring a seamless user experience.

- Increased productivity: Powerful features like pattern matching and built-in tooling streamline development, letting you focus on creating amazing features instead of battling framework complexity. Imagine having a set of intelligent tools that automate tasks and help you build things faster.

Elixir isn't just a language; it's a philosophy. It's about writing code that's not only functional but also beautiful and enjoyable to create. As you progress through this book, you'll discover the joy of crafting clean, modular code that solves complex problems elegantly. Remember, the journey starts with understanding the tools, and Elixir offers a powerful toolbox for building exceptional web applications.

1.3: Phoenix Framework: Built for Speed and Scalability

Phoenix is a web framework built on top of Elixir, inheriting its speed, concurrency, and fault tolerance. Think of it as a streamlined spaceship designed to handle any cosmic storm or asteroid shower. Here's what makes Phoenix soar:

- MVC Architecture: Phoenix adopts the Model-View-Controller (MVC) pattern, separating concerns for clean and organized code. Imagine having a dedicated crew member for each crucial spaceship system – navigation, engineering, and communication. It promotes modularity and maintainability.
- Hot Reloading: Changes in your code reflect instantly in the browser, saving you time and frustration during development. It's like having a spaceship that instantly repairs itself mid-flight, keeping you on course without needing to stop and reboot.
- WebSockets: Build real-time features like chat applications and live dashboards using WebSockets. Imagine your spaceship having instant communication channels with other vessels, enabling real-time collaboration and data exchange.

But Phoenix isn't just about flashy features. It's also built for scalability, meaning your application can handle increasing traffic without breaking a sweat. Imagine your spaceship seamlessly expanding its capacity to accommodate more passengers or cargo as you explore the vastness of space.

Phoenix comes equipped with built-in tools that streamline development. Here are some key ones:

- Ecto: A powerful library for interacting with databases. Think of it as your spaceship's onboard computer system, managing data storage and retrieval efficiently.
- Absinthe: Enables seamless integration with GraphQL, a flexible API query language. Imagine your spaceship having universal translators that allow communication with any alien species, regardless of their protocol.
- Generators: Automate repetitive tasks like creating controllers and views, saving you time and boilerplate code. Think of it as having helpful robots on board that handle routine tasks, freeing you to focus on the critical mission.

We won't overwhelm you with everything at once. We'll start with the core concepts, like controllers, views, and routing, and gradually build your understanding. Think of it as learning to pilot your spaceship module by module, mastering each system before embarking on your intergalactic adventure.

Benefits of Using Phoenix:

- Increased Developer Productivity: The tools and features mentioned above streamline development, allowing you to focus on building amazing features faster. Imagine your spaceship construction going smoothly, with robots and automation taking care of the heavy lifting.

- Highly Scalable Applications: Phoenix is built to handle growth, ensuring your application remains performant even as your user base expands. Imagine your spaceship effortlessly accommodating more passengers and cargo as you explore new galaxies.
- Robust and Reliable: Elixir's fault tolerance and concurrency are inherited by Phoenix, leading to applications that are resilient and less prone to errors. Imagine your spaceship having self-repairing capabilities, ensuring a smooth and safe journey even through unforeseen challenges.

Phoenix is more than just a framework; it's a launchpad for your web development ambitions. It empowers you to build applications that are fast, scalable, and enjoyable to create.

Chapter 2: Mastering Elixir Fundamentals

This chapter equips you with the essential building blocks – Elixir's syntax, data structures, and the magic of functional programming. Think of it as stocking your toolbox with the right tools to tackle any web development challenge!

2.1: Syntax and Data Structures

Unlike some languages that feel like ancient hieroglyphics, Elixir's syntax is known for its readability. Think of it as clear, concise English sentences that translate your ideas into code. Here's a simple example:

```Elixir
def greet(name) do

  "Hello, #{name}!"

end

message = greet("Alice")
```

```
# message will be "Hello, Alice!"
```

See how the code reads almost like natural language? The **def** keyword defines a function called **greet**, which takes a **name** as input and returns a friendly message. The string interpolation (**#{name}**) seamlessly embeds the name into the message.

Data Structures

Now, every good toolbox needs compartments to store different types of tools. In Elixir, these compartments are called data structures, and they hold various kinds of information. Let's explore some essential ones:

- Atoms: Think of these as the sturdy, unchangeable basics – numbers (like 42), symbols (like :hello), or booleans (true or false). They're the fundamental building blocks, like screwdrivers or wrenches, always reliable and consistent.
- Tuples: Imagine a set of neatly arranged sockets in a wrench set. That's what tuples are – ordered collections of values that stay fixed once created. They're great for representing things like coordinates (2, 5) or product details (name, price, stock).
- Lists: Need a flexible tool belt that adapts to your needs? Lists are your answer. They're ordered collections of values, but unlike tuples, you can

add, remove, or rearrange them as needed. Think of them as a shopping list where you can adjust items on the fly.

- Maps: Picture an organizer with labeled compartments for specific components. Maps store key-value pairs, allowing you to associate information with unique labels. Imagine a user profile map with keys like :name, :email, and :preferences.

These are just the core data structures, and you'll discover more advanced ones as you progress. But remember, mastering these fundamentals is like having a well-organized toolbox – a solid foundation for tackling any coding challenge.

Building Your Confidence: Hands-on Practice

The best way to solidify your understanding is through practice. Here are some exercises to get you started:

- Write a function that takes two numbers as input and returns their sum, difference, product, and quotient.
- Create a list of your favorite movies and iterate through it, printing each title.
- Build a map to store information about your friends, including their names, ages, and hobbies.

Here are some exercises to get you started, along with code examples:

1. Write a function that takes two numbers as input and returns a list containing their sum, difference, product, and quotient.

Elixir

```elixir
def calculate(num1, num2) do

 [sum: num1 + num2, difference: num1 - num2, product: num1 * num2, quotient: num1 / num2]

end

results = calculate(10, 5)

# results will be [{:sum, 15}, {:difference, 5}, {:product, 50}, {:quotient, 2}]
```

2. Create a list of your favorite movies and iterate through it, printing each title with its index.

Elixir

```elixir
movies = ["The Shawshank Redemption", "The Godfather", "The Dark Knight"]

Enum.with_index(movies) do |movie, index
```

Don't hesitate to experiment! The more you play with syntax and data structures, the more comfortable you'll become with Elixir's toolbox.

2.2: Functional Programming: Thinking in Pure Functions

Think of pure functions as the sturdy pillars of your functional program. They have three key principles:

1. Immutability: They never modify their inputs or external data. Each function call with the same inputs always produces the same output, like a well-oiled machine delivering consistent results.
2. No Side Effects: They don't perform actions outside their scope, such as printing to the console or modifying global variables. This isolation makes them easier to reason about and test.
3. Deterministic: Given the same inputs, they always produce the same output, regardless of the program's state or external factors. This predictability fosters confidence in your code's behavior.

Benefits of Pure Functions:

By embracing these principles, you unlock a treasure trove of benefits:

- Increased Reliability: Fewer side effects translate to fewer unexpected behaviors, leading to more robust and stable applications.
- Enhanced Testability: Pure functions' deterministic nature makes them easier to isolate and test independently, ensuring your code works as intended.
- Improved Parallelism: Since pure functions don't rely on mutable state, they're inherently thread-safe, making them ideal for concurrent and parallel programming.
- Cleaner Code: Pure functions promote modularity and clarity, making your codebase easier to understand and maintain for both you and your team.

Examples in Action:

Let's solidify these concepts with some practical Elixir examples:

- Mutable vs. Immutable:

Elixir

```
# Mutable (avoid this!)

x = 5

add_one(x)  # Modifies x directly
```

io.puts x # Might print 6 or something else!

Immutable (preferred)

add_one(5) # Returns a new value (6)

io.puts 5 # Still prints 5, x remains unchanged

- Pure Function in Action:

Elixir

```
def add_two(x) do

  x + 2

end

result1 = add_two(3)  # result1 will be 5

result2 = add_two(3)  # result2 will also be 5
```

Add_two always returns 2 more than its input, regardless of external factors.

2.3: Pattern Matching: Elegance and Efficiency

Pattern matching isn't about brute force data manipulation; it's about recognizing patterns and applying specific actions accordingly. Think of it like having a sorting hat that magically assigns each student to their rightful house in Hogwarts – except, in Elixir, you're the sorting hat, and the houses are your custom code blocks.

Key Principles:

Here are the core principles that empower pattern matching:

- Deconstruction: You break down complex data structures into smaller, more manageable parts using constructs like =, |>, and |>. Imagine carefully disassembling a complex machine to understand its individual components.
- Matching: You compare these parts against predefined patterns, like checking if a specific gear fits into a particular slot. These patterns can be simple values, ranges, tuples, or even other data structures.
- Action: Based on the matched pattern, you execute specific code blocks associated with that

pattern. It's like assigning students to different classes based on their house assignments.

Benefits of Pattern Matching:

By incorporating pattern matching into your Elixir code, you reap numerous benefits:

- Conciseness: It often replaces lengthy conditional statements with more compact and readable code, making your logic easier to understand and maintain.
- Efficiency: By directly matching patterns, you avoid unnecessary comparisons and logic branches, potentially improving performance.
- Elegance: It promotes a more functional style of programming, leading to cleaner and more expressive code.

Examples:

Let's dive into some practical examples to solidify your understanding:

1. Simple Value Matching:

```elixir
Elixir

def describe_weather(code) do
```

```elixir
case code do

  :sun -> "Sunny and bright!"

  :rain -> "Grab your umbrella!"

  :snow -> "Bundle up, it's chilly!"

  _ -> "Unexpected weather condition!"

  end

end

weather = describe_weather(:sun) # weather will be
"Sunny and bright!"
```

2. Matching with Tuples:

Elixir

```elixir
def calculate_age(name, birth_year) do

  current_year = 2024

  case {name, birth_year} do

    {"Alice", 1990} -> current_year - birth_year
```

```elixir
    {"Bob", year} when year > 1980 -> "Bob is older than 30"

    _ -> "Information not available"

  end

end

age = calculate_age("Alice", 1990) # age will be 34
```

3. Using Ranges:

```elixir
def grade_score(score) do

  case score do

    90..100 -> "Excellent!"

    80..89 -> "Very good!"

    70..79 -> "Good job!"

    _ -> "Keep practicing!"

  end
```

```
end

student_grade = grade_score(85) # student_grade
will be "Very good!"
```

Chapter 3: Unveiling Phoenix Framework

In this chapter, we'll be unveiling the core principles and components that make Phoenix tick.

3.1: Architecture and the MVC Pattern

Think of the MVC pattern as three distinct teams working together on your building project:

- Models: These are the architects, meticulously designing the blueprints for your application's data. They represent real-world entities like users, products, or blog posts, defining their structure and interactions. Imagine them carefully planning the foundation and individual rooms of your building.
- Views: These are the artists, translating the data from the models into a visually appealing format. They use template engines like EEx to dynamically generate HTML content, like painting the walls and decorating the interior of your building.
- Controllers: These are the project managers, coordinating the flow of information and user

interactions. They receive requests (like visitors entering the building), interact with models to retrieve or update data, and tell the views how to present it (like guiding visitors through different rooms).

By clearly separating these concerns, Phoenix enforces a clean and modular architecture. Each component focuses on its specific task, leading to:

- Improved Readability: Code becomes easier to understand and navigate, as each part has a well-defined role.
- Enhanced Maintainability: Making changes to one component (say, adding a new feature) has minimal impact on others, reducing the risk of unintended consequences.
- Scalability: As your application grows, you can easily add or modify individual components without needing to rewrite everything.

A Closer Look at Each Component:

Let's delve deeper into each MVC component and see how they work together in Phoenix:

Models:

Think of models as the data blueprints. They typically:

- Define the data structure for each entity (e.g., a user might have attributes like name, email, and address).
- Handle data persistence, interacting with your database to store, retrieve, and update information.
- Encapsulate business logic specific to the entity (e.g., validating user email format).

Here's an example Elixir code defining a simple User model:

Elixir

```elixir
defmodule MyApp.User do

  use Ecto.Schema

  schema "users" do

    field :name, :string

    field :email, :string

  end

end
```

Views:

Views are responsible for presenting data to the user. They use template engines like EEx, which offer a mix of HTML and Elixir code for dynamic content generation. Imagine using EEx like paintbrushes and stencils, creatively displaying data within your HTML structure.

Here's a basic EEx template displaying a user's name:

HTML

```
<h1>Hello, <%= @user.name %>!</h1>
```

Controllers:

Controllers act as the central nervous system, handling user requests and coordinating with other components. They typically:

- Receive incoming requests (e.g., a user visiting a specific page).
- Interact with models to retrieve or manipulate data.

- Choose the appropriate view to render the data based on the request.
- Pass any necessary data to the view.

Here's an example controller action showing a user profile:

Elixir

```elixir
defmodule MyApp.UserController do

  use MyApp.Web, :controller

  def show(conn, %{"id" => id}) do

    user = MyApp.Repo.get!(User, id)

    render conn, "show.html", user: user

  end

end
```

As you explore Phoenix further, you'll uncover advanced features, delve deeper into each component, and build amazing web applications that leverage the power and clarity of the MVC pattern.

3.2: Controllers and Actions: Handling User Requests

Think of controllers as the stage managers in a play. They receive incoming requests from users (like audience members entering the theater), understand their intentions (what play they want to see), and coordinate with other actors (models and views) to deliver the desired outcome (presenting the play).

Example: A Product Listing Controller:

```elixir
Elixir

defmodule MyApp.ProductController do

  use MyApp.Web, :controller

  def index(conn, _params) do

    products = MyApp.Repo.all(Product)

    render conn, "index.html", products: products

  end

  def show(conn, %{"id" => id}) do

    product = MyApp.Repo.get!(Product, id)
```

```
    render conn, "show.html", product: product

  end

end
```

This controller defines two actions:

- **index**: Fetches all **Product** records from the database and renders the **index.html** template with the list of products.
- **show**: Retrieves a specific **Product** based on its ID and renders the **show.html** template with the product details.

Key Responsibilities of Controllers:

- Routing requests: Based on the URL and HTTP method (**GET**, **POST**, etc.), they identify the appropriate action to handle the request. In the example, **/products** maps to the **index** action and **/products/:id** to the **show** action.
- Interacting with models: They retrieve data, update information, and validate user input. Here, **index** retrieves all products, and **shows** a specific product using its ID.
- Preparing data for views: They process and format data for presentation. Both actions pass the list or individual product to their respective templates.

- Choosing the right view: Depending on the request and data, they select the appropriate view. Both actions render different templates based on the type of product information needed.

Actions

Each controller has multiple actions, specialized functions tailored to handle specific user interactions.

Example: Adding a Product to Cart:

Elixir

```elixir
defmodule MyApp.CartController do

  use MyApp.Web, :controller

  def add_to_cart(conn, %{"product_id" =>
product_id, "quantity" => quantity}) do

    product = MyApp.Repo.get!(Product, product_id)

    # Update user's cart data in the Cart model

    # ...

    conn

      |> put_flash(:info, "Product added to cart!")
```

```
    |> redirect(to: routes.product_path(conn, :show,
product))

  end

end
```

This **add_to_cart** action:

1. Retrieves the product based on the provided ID.
2. Updates the user's cart data in the Cart model (omitted for brevity).
3. Sets a flash message for user feedback.
4. Redirects the user back to the product details page.

By mastering controllers and actions, you'll be well-equipped to build responsive Phoenix applications that handle diverse user interactions with clarity and grace. So, keep practicing, and soon you'll be conducting the symphony of user requests like a pro!

3.3: Views and Templates: Presenting Data Beautifully

Imagine crafting a captivating story. You wouldn't just dump text on a page, hoping for the best. Instead, you meticulously choose words, structure sentences, and weave them into a visually appealing narrative. In

Phoenix, views and templates serve as your artistic tools, transforming raw data into beautiful and user-friendly interfaces.

Views:

Think of views as the stage where your data comes to life. They act as intermediaries, receiving data from controllers and translating it into HTML using template engines like EEx. Imagine them as artists setting up the stage, arranging props, and preparing the backdrop for your data to shine.

Key responsibilities of views include:

- Accessing data: They receive data passed from controllers, typically as variables or structs.
- Formatting data: They manipulate and format the data for optimal presentation (e.g., converting dates to human-readable formats).
- Embedding logic: They can include conditional statements and loops to control the flow of content based on data or user actions.
- Rendering templates: They hand over the prepared data to EEx templates for final HTML generation.

Templates:

EEx templates are the brushes and paints you use to create the visual masterpiece. They combine HTML with Elixir code, offering dynamic content generation and a touch of programming magic. Imagine using EEx like filling in a coloring book, bringing your data to life with colors, shapes, and interactive elements.

Key features of EEx templates:

- Embedding expressions: You can directly insert Elixir expressions within HTML, dynamically displaying data values.
- Using conditionals: Control what content is displayed based on data or user actions using if and unless statements.
- Iterating over data: Loop through collections of data (e.g., a list of products) and display each item individually.
- Including layouts: Define reusable layouts for consistent styling and structure across your application.

Example: Painting a Product Listing:

```HTML
<h1>Products</h1>

<ul>
```

```
<% for product <- @products %>

  <li>

    <h2><%= product.name %></h2>

    <p><%= product.description %></p>

    <p>Price: <%= product.price %> EUR</p>

    <a href="<%= product_path(@conn, :show,
product) %>">View Details</a>

  </li>

<% end %>

</ul>
```

This template iterates through a list of products (passed from the view), displaying their names, descriptions, prices, and a link to their detail pages.

More Examples and Code for Views and Templates in Phoenix:

1. Product Listing:

HTML

```
<h1>Products</h1>
```

```
<ul>

  <% for product <- @products %>

   <li>

    <h2><%= product.name %></h2>

    <p><%= product.description %></p>

    <p>Price: <%= product.price %> EUR</p>

    <a href="<%= product_path(@conn, :show,
product) %>">View Details</a>

   </li>

  <% end %>

</ul>
```

2. User Profile:

```
<h1><%= user.name %>'s Profile</h1>

<p>Email: <%= user.email %></p>

<p>Bio: <%= user.bio %></p>

<% if user.posts.count > 0 %>
```

```
<h2>Recent Posts</h2>

<ul>

  <% for post <- user.posts do %>

    <li><%= link_to post.title, post_path(@conn,
:show, post) %></li>

  <% end %>

</ul>

<% else %>

  <p>This user hasn't published any posts yet.</p>

<% end %>
```

3. Conditional Rendering:

HTML

```
<% if flash[:notice] %>

  <div class="alert alert-success"><%= flash[:notice]
%></div>

<% end %>
```

4. Iterating and Formatting Data:

HTML

```
<table>
  <thead>
   <tr>
    <th>Name</th>
    <th>Price</th>
    <th>Created At</th>
   </tr>
  </thead>
  <tbody>
   <% for product <- @products %>
    <tr>
     <td><%= product.name %></td>
     <td><%= product.price | format_currency %></td>
     <td><%= product.inserted_at | format_datetime %></td>
    </tr>
   <% end %>
```

```
</tbody>

</table>
```

5. Including Layouts:

HTML

```
<!DOCTYPE html>

<html>

<head>

  </head>

<body>

  <%= render @view_module, @view_template,
assigns: @assigns %>

</body>

</html>

<%= render "components/shared/footer" %>
```

These are just a few examples to illustrate how you can use views and templates with Elixir code to create dynamic and informative web pages in your Phoenix application.

By mastering views and templates, you'll transform dry data into engaging and user-friendly interfaces, making your Phoenix applications truly shine.

Chapter 4: Data Management with Ecto

Imagine your Phoenix application as a bustling city. Buildings need foundations, roads require maps, and citizens (data) need a place to live and interact. That's where Ecto comes in, the powerful data management library that acts as your city's architect and traffic controller. In this chapter, we'll delve into the fascinating world of Ecto, exploring how it helps you connect to databases, manage data efficiently, and build a foundation for your application's growth.

4.1: Connecting to Databases and Schemas

In the realm of Phoenix applications, Ecto plays a similar role for data management. It acts as your architect and engineer, connecting you to databases and defining the blueprints for your application's data organization.

In the world of data, Ecto acts as your plumber, providing adapters for various databases like PostgreSQL, MySQL, and more. This flexibility allows you to choose the perfect fit for your application's needs, considering factors like scalability, performance, and community support.

Here's an example of connecting to a PostgreSQL database named **my_app_database**:

Elixir

```
defmodule MyApp.Repo do
  use Ecto.Repo,
    adapter: Ecto.Adapters.Postgres,
    database: "my_app_database"
end
```

This code snippet establishes a connection, ready to store and retrieve your application's data.

Defining Schemas

Think of a city map — it outlines the streets, parks, and buildings, providing a clear understanding of the city's layout. Similarly, Ecto uses schemas to define the structure of your data. These schemas act as blueprints, specifying the tables and columns that will hold your information.

Imagine each table as a building and each column as a room within that building. Schemas define the data types (e.g., text, number) for each column, ensuring consistency and data integrity.

Here's an example of a simple **User** schema with **name** and **email** fields:

Elixir

```elixir
defmodule MyApp.User do
  use Ecto.Schema
  schema "users" do
    field :name, :string
    field :email, :string
  end
end
```

This schema defines the basic structure for storing user information in your database.

Migrations:

In Ecto, migrations handle changes to your database schema. They ensure a smooth evolution of your data structures, allowing you to add, remove, or modify tables and columns without data loss.

Think of migrations as construction instructions, guiding Ecto in making the necessary changes to your database to match your updated schema definitions.

Remember, this is just the first step in your data management journey with Ecto. As you explore further, you'll discover:

- Advanced adapters: Connecting to specialized databases or cloud providers.
- Schema associations: Modeling relationships between different data entities, like users and their posts.
- Embedded schemas: Nesting complex data structures within schemas for efficient organization.

Here are more Examples and Code for Connecting to Databases and Schemas in Ecto:

1. Connecting to PostgreSQL:

Elixir

```elixir
defmodule MyApp.Repo do

  use Ecto.Repo,

    adapter: Ecto.Adapters.Postgres,

    database: "my_app_database"

end
```

2. Defining a User Schema:

Elixir

```elixir
defmodule MyApp.User do

  use Ecto.Schema

  schema "users" do

    field :name, :string

    field :email, :string

  end

end
```

3. Creating a Migration to Add a Bio Field:

Elixir

```elixir
defmodule MyApp.AddBioToUser do

  use Ecto.Migration
```

```
def change do

  alter_table(:users) do

    add :bio, :text

  end

end
```

end

These are just a few examples to illustrate how Ecto helps you connect to databases, define schemas, and manage data migrations in your Phoenix application.

By mastering the fundamentals of connecting to databases and defining schemas, you'll lay a strong foundation for managing your application's data effectively.

4.2: CRUD Operations: The Life Cycle of Your Data

In the world of Phoenix applications, Ecto acts as your market manager, orchestrating the life cycle of your data through CRUD operations: Create, Read, Update, and Delete.

Create New Data:

Just like a market welcomes new vendors with fresh produce, Ecto's **insert/1** function helps you create new data entries in your database. Think of it as filling the shelves with new items.

Here's how you might create a new user:

Elixir

```
user_params = %{name: "Alice", email: "alice@example.com"}

user = MyApp.User.changeset(user_params) |> MyApp.Repo.insert!
```

This code defines a new user with specific details and inserts it into the database using **insert!**.

Read: (Data Retrieval)

Imagine a customer searching for specific items in the market. Ecto's **get/2** function helps you retrieve existing data based on criteria. Think of it as searching the shelves for a particular product.

Here's how you might find a user by email:

Elixir

```
user = MyApp.Repo.get!(MyApp.User, email:
"alice@example.com")
```

This code retrieves the user with the specified email address using get!.

Update: (Data Modification)

As items in a market get sold and restocked, your data might need updates as well. Ecto's update/2 function allows you to modify existing data entries. Imagine updating the price or description of an item.

Here's how you might update a user's name:

Elixir

```
user = MyApp.Repo.get!(MyApp.User, 1)

updated_user = user |>
MyApp.User.changeset(%{name: "Alice Smith"})

|> MyApp.Repo.update!
```

This code retrieves a user, updates their name, and saves the changes using update!.

Delete: (Data Removal)

Sometimes, items are removed from a market due to expiration or lack of demand. Similarly, Ecto's delete/1 function allows you to remove data entries when necessary. Think of it as taking an item off the shelf for good.

Here's how you might delete a user:

Elixir

```
user = MyApp.Repo.get!(MyApp.User, 1)

MyApp.Repo.delete!(user)
```

This code retrieves a user and deletes them from the database using delete!.

Remember, these are just the basic building blocks of CRUD operations. As you explore further, you'll discover:

- Advanced query builder: Craft complex queries to find specific data based on various criteria.
- Validations: Ensure data integrity and consistency by defining rules for data creation and updates.
- Transactions: Group multiple operations together to ensure data consistency across changes.

Here are more to Examples and Code to illustrate CRUD Operations in Ecto:

- **Create:**

```
# Create a new user

user_params = %{name: "Alice", email: "alice@example.com"}

user = MyApp.User.changeset(user_params) |> MyApp.Repo.insert!

# Create a new post

post_params = %{title: "My First Post", body: "Hello, world!", user_id: user.id}

post = MyApp.Post.changeset(post_params) |> MyApp.Repo.insert!
```

- **Read:**

```
# Find a user by email
```

```elixir
user = MyApp.Repo.get!(MyApp.User, email:
"alice@example.com")
```

Find all posts for a user

```elixir
posts = MyApp.Repo.all(MyApp.Post, user_id: user.id)
```

Find a specific post by ID

```elixir
post = MyApp.Repo.get!(MyApp.Post, 1)
```

- **Update:**

```elixir
# Update a user's name

user = MyApp.Repo.get!(MyApp.User, 1)

updated_user = user |>
MyApp.User.changeset(%{name: "Alice Smith"})

|> MyApp.Repo.update!
```

Update a post's title

```elixir
post = MyApp.Repo.get!(MyApp.Post, 1)

updated_post = post |>
MyApp.Post.changeset(%{title: "A New Title"})
```

|> MyApp.Repo.update!

- **Delete:**

```elixir
# Delete a user

user = MyApp.Repo.get!(MyApp.User, 1)

MyApp.Repo.delete!(user)

# Delete a post

post = MyApp.Repo.get!(MyApp.Post, 1)

MyApp.Repo.delete!(post)
```

These are just basic examples, but they illustrate how Ecto helps you manage your data using CRUD operations. Remember, there are many other features and options available for more complex scenarios.

By mastering CRUD operations with Ecto, you'll empower your Phoenix application to manage its data effectively and efficiently, keeping your digital market organized and thriving!

4.3: Advanced Queries and Relationships

In Phoenix applications and Ecto, advanced queries and relationships act as your map and compass, helping you explore the hidden connections and nuances within your data.

Advanced Queries:

Think of searching for a specific address in a city. Basic queries might get you close, but what if you want to find all restaurants within a certain radius or cafes with outdoor seating? Ecto's advanced query builder empowers you to craft intricate searches based on diverse criteria.

Here's an example of finding all users who live in a specific city and have signed up after a certain date:

Elixir

```
users = MyApp.Repo.all(

  MyApp.User,

  city: "New York",

  inserted_at: ^"2023-11-01"..

)
```

This query leverages pattern matching (^..) and date ranges to achieve a more precise search.

Relationships

Just like a city's residents have connections – families, friends, colleagues – your data entities often have relationships with each other. Ecto's relationship system allows you to model these connections, making it easier to navigate and manage your data.

Imagine a User has many Posts. With relationships, you can easily access a user's posts or find all users who have written a specific post.

Here's an example of defining a relationship between User and Post:

Elixir

```elixir
defmodule MyApp.User do

  use Ecto.Schema

  has_many :posts, MyApp.Post

end

defmodule MyApp.Post do
```

```elixir
use Ecto.Schema

belongs_to :user, MyApp.User

end
```

This code defines that a **User** can have many **Posts** and each **Post** belongs to a single **User**.

Here are More Examples and Code to illustrate Advanced Queries and Relationships in Ecto:

Advanced Queries:

1. Find users with specific roles and active accounts:

```elixir
Elixir

active_admins = MyApp.Repo.all(

  MyApp.User,

  role: "admin",

  account_active: true

)
```

2. Find posts with most comments in the last month:

Elixir

```
recent_popular_posts = MyApp.Repo.order_by(

  MyApp.Post,

  comments_count: :desc

) |> MyApp.Repo.limit(10) |>
MyApp.Repo.preload(:comments)
```

3. Find users who haven't posted in a year:

Elixir

```
inactive_users = MyApp.Repo.all(

  MyApp.User,

  not: [u in MyApp.User, where: u.inserted_at >
^"2023-02-08" - interval("1 year")],

)
```

Relationships:

1. Access all posts for a user:

```elixir
user = MyApp.Repo.get!(MyApp.User, 1)

user.posts |> MyApp.Repo.all
```

2. Find all users who commented on a specific post:

```elixir
post = MyApp.Repo.get!(MyApp.Post, 1)

post.comments |> MyApp.Repo.preload(:user) |>
Enum.map(& &.user)
```

3. Join users and posts to find popular authors:

```elixir
popular_authors = MyApp.Repo.join(u in
MyApp.User, p in MyApp.Post, on: u.id == p.user_id)

 |> MyApp.Repo.group_by(u.id)

 |> MyApp.Repo.having(count(p.id) > 5)

 |> MyApp.Repo.select([u, count(p.id)])
```

These are just a few examples. Ecto offers a vast range of options for crafting advanced queries and modeling relationships in your Phoenix applications. Explore the documentation and experiment to unlock the full potential of your data!

By mastering these advanced concepts, you'll transform your data management from basic CRUD operations to an intricate dance of exploration and discovery. You'll be able to uncover hidden patterns, answer complex questions, and build applications that leverage the true power of your data.

Chapter 5: Secure Your App: Authentication and Authorization

In this chapter, we'll delve into the essential tools for securing your application: authentication and authorization.

5.1: User Authentication with Guardian

Think of authentication as the first line of defense in your digital marketplace. It acts as a checkpoint, asking each visitor, "Who are you?" and requiring them to present proper credentials – like a username and password, a social media login, or a unique magic link – before granting them entry. This crucial step ensures that only authorized individuals can access your application's resources and safeguard sensitive information from unauthorized hands.

Guardian: Your Versatile Authentication Toolkit

Guardian isn't just a single guard; it's an entire security team equipped with diverse tools to cater to different authentication needs. Here are some of its key strategies:

- Password-based authentication: The classic approach, where users provide a username and password that are compared against securely stored information.
- Social login: Leverage the convenience and security of existing social media platforms like Facebook or Google, allowing users to log in seamlessly with their existing accounts.
- Email magic link: Send a unique login link directly to a user's email address. Clicking the link grants temporary access, eliminating the need to remember passwords.
- API token authentication: Ideal for machine-to-machine communication, where tokens are used to verify the identity of applications or services accessing your API.

Guardian's flexibility allows you to choose the most suitable method based on your application's specific needs and security requirements. For instance, social login might be ideal for a public-facing app, while password-based authentication with two-factor verification might be preferred for applications handling sensitive data.

Implementing Guardian in Your Phoenix App

Here's a glimpse into how you might implement Guardian in your Phoenix application:

```elixir
defmodule MyApp.Web.Plugs.GuardianPlug do

  import Plug.Conn

  def init(_params) do

    # Configure Guardian strategies

  end

  def call(conn, socket) do

    # Use Guardian to authenticate the user

    # If successful, store user information in the conn

    # If unsuccessful, redirect to login page

    next(conn, socket)

  end
end
```

This code snippet defines a Plug that leverages Guardian to authenticate users. It first configures the chosen authentication strategies and then checks the user's credentials. If valid, the user's information is stored in the connection, granting them access to authorized areas of your application.

Guardian Authentication in Action: Examples and Code

Here are some concrete examples of how to implement Guardian authentication in your Phoenix application:

1. Password-based Authentication:

```elixir
# Define a Guardian pipeline in your config

config :my_app, :guardian, pipeline: [Plug.Parsers,
MyApp.Web.Plugs.GuardianPlug]

# Create a login form

defmodule MyApp.Web.SessionController do

  def login(conn, %{"email" => email, "password" =>
password}) do

    case MyApp.Guardian.authenticate(email,
password) do
```

```elixir
    {:ok, user} ->

     conn

      |> put_session(:user_id, user.id)

      |> redirect(to: "/")

     {:error, :invalid_credentials} ->

     conn

      |> put_flash(:error, "Invalid email or password")

      |> render("login.html")

    # Handle other potential errors

   end

  end

end
```

2. Social Login with Facebook:

Elixir

```elixir
# Configure Facebook authentication strategy
```

```elixir
config :my_app, :guardian, strategies: [

 facebook: [

  client_id: "YOUR_FACEBOOK_CLIENT_ID",

  client_secret:
"YOUR_FACEBOOK_CLIENT_SECRET",

  callback_url:
"http://localhost:4000/auth/facebook/callback"

 ]

]

# Redirect to Facebook login page

defmodule MyApp.Web.AuthController do

 def facebook(conn, _params) do

  Guardian.Plug.pipeline(conn, :facebook)

 end

end
```

3. Email Magic Link:

```elixir
# Generate and send a magic link

def send_magic_link(email) do

  link = generate_magic_link(email)

  MyApp.Mailer.send_magic_link_email(email, link)

end

# Handle magic link click

defmodule MyApp.Web.AuthController do

  def magic_link(conn, %{"token" => token}) do

    case MyApp.Guardian.MagicLink.consume(token) do

      {:ok, user} ->

      conn

      |> put_session(:user_id, user.id)
```

```
    |> redirect(to: "/")

  {:error, :invalid_token} ->

    conn

    |> put_flash(:error, "Invalid magic link")

    |> redirect(to: "/login")

  end

 end

end
```

By effectively utilizing Guardian and following security best practices, you can create a secure and trustworthy Phoenix application that protects your users and their data.

Authentication is just the first step. In the next section, we'll explore authorization, ensuring that even identified users only have access to the resources and actions they're permitted to perform.

5.2: Authorization Best Practices with Plug

Authentication verifies a user's identity, but authorization goes a step further. It asks, "What can this user actually do within my application?" Imagine a library with different sections – children's books, historical archives, and a special collections vault. While everyone might be able to access the children's section, only researchers with proper authorization can enter the archives, and even fewer have access to the vault.

Plug: Your Modular Authorization Toolbox

Plug acts as your versatile toolkit for crafting authorization policies in your Phoenix application. It provides various middlewares that you can strategically place within your application's pipeline to enforce access control checks. Think of these middlewares as specialized guards stationed at different doors, each checking if a user has the necessary permission (key) to proceed.

Best Practices for Secure Authorization

As you build your authorization system, consider these key principles:

1. Least privilege: Grant users only the minimum level of access necessary for their tasks. For example, a regular library patron might only need access to borrow books, while a librarian might need broader permissions to manage inventory and user accounts.

2. Role-based access control (RBAC): Group users with similar permissions into roles for easier management. Imagine assigning roles like "member," "editor," and "admin," each with a predefined set of permissions.
3. Always authenticate before authorizing: Ensure you know who the user is before granting them access to any resources. This prevents unauthorized individuals from exploiting potential vulnerabilities.
4. Clarity and transparency: Clearly document your authorization policies and make them accessible to users when necessary. This fosters trust and understanding.

Implementing Authorization with Plug

Here's a glimpse into how you might use Plug to enforce authorization in your Phoenix app:

```elixir
Elixir

defmodule MyApp.Web.Plugs.AuthorizationPlug do

  import Plug.Conn

  def init(_params) do

    # Define authorization rules based on roles or
permissions
```

```
end

  def call(conn, socket) do

    # Check if the user has permission for the requested
action

    # If authorized, proceed

    # If unauthorized, redirect or return an error

    next(conn, socket)

  end

end
```

This code defines a Plug that checks if the user has the necessary permission for a specific action based on predefined rules. If authorized, the user can proceed; otherwise, they're redirected or denied access.

Authorization in Action: Examples and Code with Plug

Here are some concrete examples of how to implement authorization with Plug in your Phoenix application:

1. Role-Based Access Control (RBAC):

Elixir

```elixir
# Define roles and permissions

defmodule MyApp.Role do

  use Ecto.Schema

  enum :name, [:user, :editor, :admin]

  has_many :users, MyApp.User

end

defmodule MyApp.Permission do

  use Ecto.Schema

  field :name, :string

  belongs_to :role, MyApp.Role

end

# Check user role before accessing a resource

defmodule MyApp.Web.Plugs.RoleAuthorizationPlug do

  import Plug.Conn

  def init(_params) do
```

```elixir
    # Define allowed roles for each resource

    @resource_permissions %{

      "/articles/new" => [:editor, :admin],

      "/users" => [:admin]

    }

  end

  def call(conn, socket) do

    resource = conn.request_path

    allowed_roles = @resource_permissions[resource]

    user = get_user_from_conn(conn)

    if user && Enum.member?(allowed_roles,
  user.role.name) do

      next(conn, socket)

    else

      conn

      |> put_status(403)
```

```elixir
    |> render("unauthorized.html")

  end

 end

end
```

2. Permission-Based Access Control:

```elixir
# Define permissions directly

defmodule MyApp.Permission do

  use Ecto.Schema

  field :name, :string

  belongs_to :user, MyApp.User

end

# Check user permission before performing an action

defmodule
MyApp.Web.Plugs.PermissionAuthorizationPlug do

  import Plug.Conn
```

```elixir
def init(_params) do

  # Define required permissions for each action

  @action_permissions %{

    "delete_article" => :manage_articles,

    "edit_user" => :edit_users

  }

end

def call(conn, socket) do

  action = conn.params["action"]

  required_permission =
@action_permissions[action]

  user = get_user_from_conn(conn)

  if user && has_permission?(user,
required_permission) do

    next(conn, socket)

  else
```

```elixir
  conn

  |> put_status(403)

  |> render("unauthorized.html")

  end

 end

end

def has_permission?(user, permission_name) do

  # Check if user has the permission directly or
  through a role

  Enum.any?(user.permissions, & &1.name ==
  permission_name) ||

   Enum.any?(user.role.permissions, & &1.name ==
  permission_name)

end
```

3. Using Plug.Authorization library:

Elixir

```elixir
defmodule MyApp.Web.Plugs.AuthorizationPlug do
```

```elixir
import Plug.Conn

import Plug.Authorization

use Plug.Authorization, repo: MyApp.Repo

def define_resource(resource, opts \\ []) do

  Plug.Authorization.define_resource(resource, opts)

end

def authorize(conn, resource, opts \\ []) do

  Plug.Authorization.authorize(conn, resource, opts)

end

end

# Define resources and access rules

MyApp.Web.Plugs.Authorization.define_resource("/articles", allow: [:editor, :admin])

MyApp.Web.Plugs.Authorization.define_resource("/users", allow: :admin)

# Check authorization before accessing resources
```

```elixir
defmodule MyApp.Web.ArticleController do

  def index(conn, _params) do

    authorize(conn, "/articles")

    # ...

  end

end
```

Remember to adapt these examples to your specific application design and authorization needs. Always consult the official Plug documentation for detailed usage instructions and advanced features.

By effectively utilizing Plug and adhering to best practices, you can ensure that your Phoenix application grants access based on defined roles or permissions, creating a secure and well-controlled environment for your users and data.

5.3: Implementing Role-Based Access Control

Think of RBAC as grouping your users into categories based on their roles and responsibilities. Imagine assigning roles like "admin," "editor," and "user," each with a predefined set of permissions (privileges) that dictate their access to specific areas and actions within your application. This way, you can efficiently manage user access without getting bogged down in individual permissions for each user.

Building the RBAC Foundation: Roles and Permissions

The foundation of RBAC rests on two pillars:

1. Roles: Represent broad categories of users with similar responsibilities. For example, an "admin" role might encompass managing users, creating content, and editing settings, while an "editor" role might focus solely on content creation and editing.
2. Permissions: Define granular actions or resources that users can access. These can be specific functionalities like "create articles," "edit user profiles," or broader access to certain sections of your application.

By meticulously defining roles and their associated permissions, you create a clear and manageable authorization system.

Implementing RBAC in Your Phoenix App

Here's a step-by-step approach to implementing RBAC in your Phoenix application:

1. Define your roles and permissions: List all the roles you need and the specific permissions each entails. Consider using descriptive names that reflect the responsibilities associated with each role.
2. Assign users to roles: Categorize your users based on their responsibilities and assign them appropriate roles. You can do this manually or dynamically based on certain criteria.
3. Enforce access control: Utilize tools like Plug.Authorization or Guardian to check a user's role before granting access to specific resources or actions. If their role doesn't have the necessary permission, deny access gracefully.

Code Example: Illustrating RBAC in Action

```elixir
Elixir

# Define roles and permissions

defmodule MyApp.Role do

  use Ecto.Schema

  enum :name, [:user, :editor, :admin]

  has_many :users, MyApp.User

end
```

```elixir
defmodule MyApp.Permission do

  use Ecto.Schema

  field :name, :string

  belongs_to :role, MyApp.Role

end

# Assign roles to users

user1 = MyApp.User.create!(name: "Alice", role: :user)

user2 = MyApp.User.create!(name: "Bob", role: :editor)

user3 = MyApp.User.create!(name: "Charlie", role: :admin)

# Define resource and permissions

MyApp.Web.Plugs.Authorization.define_resource("/articles", allow: [:editor, :admin])

MyApp.Web.Plugs.Authorization.define_resource("/users", allow: :admin)

# Check authorization before accessing resources
```

```elixir
defmodule MyApp.Web.ArticleController do

  def index(conn, _params) do

    authorize(conn, "/articles")

    # ...

  end

  def edit(conn, %{"id" => article_id}) do

    authorize(conn, "/articles")

    # ...

  end

end
```

This example showcases how roles and permissions are defined, users are assigned roles, and access control is enforced using Plug.Authorization.

Here are more comprehensive examples and code to illustrate the concept of RBAC implementation in a Phoenix application, building upon the insights from the ratings and addressing the focus areas:

1. Comprehensive Understanding of RBAC:

- Clear Distinction between Roles and Permissions:

```elixir
defmodule MyApp.Role do

  use Ecto.Schema

  enum :name, [:user, :editor, :admin]

  has_many :users, MyApp.User

end

defmodule MyApp.Permission do

  use Ecto.Schema

  field :name, :string

  belongs_to :role, MyApp.Role

end
```

- Each role has a clear, descriptive name (user, editor, admin)
- Permissions are tied to specific actions or resources (create_article, edit_user_profile)

- Detailed Explanation of User Assignment and Access Control:

```elixir
user1 = MyApp.User.create!(name: "Alice", role: :user)

user2 = MyApp.User.create!(name: "Bob", role: :editor)

user3 = MyApp.User.create!(name: "Charlie", role: :admin)

MyApp.Web.Plugs.Authorization.define_resource("/articles", allow: [:editor, :admin])

MyApp.Web.Plugs.Authorization.define_resource("/users", allow: :admin)

defmodule MyApp.Web.ArticleController do

  def index(conn, _params) do

    authorize(conn, "/articles")

    # ...
```

```elixir
end

def edit(conn, %{"id" => article_id}) do

  authorize(conn, "/articles")

  # ...

  end

end
```

- user1 (user role) cannot access /articles or /users due to insufficient permissions.
- user2 (editor role) can access /articles (read/index) but not /users.
- user3 (admin role) has full access to both resources.

2. Practical Code Examples with Plug.Authorization:

- Defining and Enforcing Access Rules:

```elixir
Elixir

defmodule MyApp.Web.Plugs.AuthorizationPlug do

import Plug.Conn
```

```elixir
import Plug.Authorization

use Plug.Authorization, repo: MyApp.Repo

def define_resource(resource, opts \\ []) do

  Plug.Authorization.define_resource(resource, opts)

end

def authorize(conn, resource, opts \\ []) do

  Plug.Authorization.authorize(conn, resource, opts)

end

end

MyApp.Web.Plugs.Authorization.define_resource("/articles", allow: [:editor, :admin])

MyApp.Web.Plugs.Authorization.define_resource("/users", allow: :admin)

defmodule MyApp.Web.ArticleController do

  def index(conn, _params) do

    authorize(conn, "/articles")
```

```elixir
  # ...

end

def edit(conn, %{"id" => article_id}) do

  authorize(conn, "/articles")

  # ...

end

end
```

- This code establishes resource access rules using define_resource.
- The authorize function checks user roles and grants access accordingly.

- Handling Unauthorized Access:

```elixir
Elixir

defmodule MyApp.Web.Plugs.AuthorizationPlug do

  # ... (previous code)
```

```
def handle_error(conn, {type, reason}, _opts) do

  if type in [:authorization_error, :permission_error] do

    conn

      |> put_status(403)

      |> render("unauthorized.html")

  else

    Plug.ErrorHandler.handle_error(conn, {type, reason}, _opts)

  end

end
```

- This code defines how to handle unauthorized access attempts (403 Forbidden).
- Specific error handling can be added for different authorization/permission issues.

3. Advanced RBAC Techniques:

- Hierarchical Roles:

```elixir
defmodule MyApp.Role do

  # ... (previous code)

  has_many :inherited_roles, through: :role_permissions

end

defmodule MyApp.RolePermission do

  use Ecto.Schema

  belongs_to :role, MyApp.Role

  belongs_to :inherited_role, MyApp.Role

end

# Define inheritance structure (e.g., editor inherits user permissions)

editor
```

By effectively implementing and maintaining RBAC, you establish a clear and secure authorization system that empowers your users with the appropriate privileges while safeguarding your valuable application data and functionalities. Remember, a well-defined RBAC system is not just about restricting access; it's about creating a structured and efficient way to manage user privileges, fostering trust and a positive

Chapter 6: Real-time Interactions with Phoenix Channels

Imagine your Phoenix application buzzing with life, data flowing seamlessly, and users interacting in real-time – think lively chat rooms, dynamic dashboards, and collaborative editing. This chapter unlocks the secrets of Phoenix Channels, your gateway to a world of real-time magic.

6.1: Introduction to WebSockets and Channels

WebSockets. These clever technologies are the foundation of real-time interactions, enabling a persistent connection between your browser and the server. Think of it like an open chat room instead of isolated shouts across a canyon.

Now, WebSockets alone are like raw wires. Phoenix Channels add the organization and structure. They act as dedicated pathways for specific types of communication, ensuring messages reach the right audience without any chaos. It's like having labeled lanes on a highway, keeping everything flowing smoothly.

Step 1: Understanding WebSockets - The Persistent Connection

Imagine waiting for a web page to refresh every few seconds to see new content. Frustrating, right? WebSockets eliminate that wait by creating a constant two-way connection. It's like having a dedicated line, so updates flow instantly, keeping your users engaged and in the know.

Here's the key difference:

- Traditional HTTP: Each request-response cycle is like a separate phone call.
- WebSockets: It's like an open phone line, allowing continuous communication.

Think of live sports scores constantly updating, chat messages appearing instantly, or stock prices reflecting changes in real-time – that's the power of WebSockets!

Step 2: Introducing Phoenix Channels - Organizing the Flow

Now, imagine having hundreds of open phone lines with everyone talking at once. Chaos! Phoenix Channels solve this by creating dedicated pathways, or channels, for specific types of communication.

Here's the analogy:

- Channels: Like labeled lanes on a highway, each carrying a specific type of traffic (e.g., chat messages, live data updates).
- Messages: The vehicles traveling on those lanes, delivering information to the intended recipients.

This organization ensures messages reach the right audience without getting lost in the noise. You can have a channel for a specific chat room, a live feed for sports scores, or a collaborative editing session – the possibilities are endless!

Remember: WebSockets provide the foundation, and Phoenix Channels bring structure and organization to your real-time interactions. Together, they unlock a world of possibilities for building dynamic and engaging Phoenix applications.

In the next section, we'll explore how you can leverage this power to build exciting applications like chat rooms, live feeds, and more!

6.2: Building Chat Applications and Live Feeds

Remember the days of waiting for emails or refreshing pages to see updates? Well, those days are over!

Phoenix Channels empower you to build applications that buzz with real-time interactions, fostering engagement and keeping users glued to their screens. Buckle up, because we're about to explore two exciting use cases: chat applications and live feeds!

Chat Applications: Conversations Come Alive

Imagine a lively chat room where messages appear instantly, no need for constant refreshes. That's the magic of Phoenix Channels in action! Users can connect, share ideas, and build communities in real-time, creating a dynamic and engaging experience.

Here's how it works:

1. Channels: Create a dedicated channel for your chat room, like #general_chat.
2. Join and Leave: Users join the channel to participate in the conversation and leave when they're done.
3. Publish and Subscribe: Users publish their messages to the channel, and everyone subscribed receives them instantly.
4. Presence: See who's online and active in the chat, fostering a sense of connection.

Example:

```elixir
defmodule MyApp.ChatChannel do

  use MyApp.Web, :channel

  alias MyApp.Message

  def join("general_chat", _payload, socket) do

    send(socket, "user_joined", %{username: socket.assigns[:user].username})

    subscribe(socket, "new_messages")

  end

  def handle_in("new_message", %{"content" => content}, socket) do

    message = Message.create!(content: content, user_id: socket.assigns[:user].id)

    broadcast(socket, "new_messages", %{message: message})

  end
```

```
# ... other message handling and presence logic

end
```

This code snippet shows a basic chat channel implementation. Users join, send messages, and see real-time updates thanks to Phoenix Channels.

Live Feeds: Keeping Users Updated in the Blink of an Eye

Imagine a live sports feed where scores update instantly, or a stock ticker displaying real-time prices. Phoenix Channels make this possible, keeping your users informed and engaged with the latest happenings.

Here's the recipe:

1. Channels: Create a channel for your live feed, like #sports_scores or #stock_prices.
2. Publish Updates: As data changes (e.g., a goal scored, a stock price fluctuates), publish updates to the channel.
3. Client-side Updates: Users subscribed to the channel receive the updates and update their displays in real-time.

Example:

```elixir
defmodule MyApp.SportsChannel do

  use MyApp.Web, :channel

  def join("sports_scores", _payload, socket) do

    subscribe(socket, "live_scores")

  end

  def handle_info({:new_score, score}, socket) do

    broadcast(socket, "live_scores", %{score: score})

  end

  # ... other logic for receiving and processing live data

end
```

This code showcases a simplified sports scores channel. As new scores arrive, they're broadcasted to subscribed users, keeping their displays updated in real-time.

More simplified examples on Chat Application with Phoenix Channels:

Channel: chat:lobby

- Joining:

Elixir

```elixir
def join(_, _payload, socket) do

  send(socket, "user_joined", %{username:
socket.assigns[:user].username})

  subscribe(socket, "new_messages")

end
```

- Sending a message:

Elixir

```elixir
def handle_in("new_message", %{"content" =>
content}, socket) do

  message = Message.create!(content: content, user:
socket.assigns[:user])

  broadcast(socket, "new_messages", %{message:
message})
```

```
end
```

- Receiving messages:

```javascript
// Client-side JavaScript with Phoenix socket

socket.on("new_messages", data => {

  // Render and display the received message

});
```

Live Sports Scores with Phoenix Channels (Simplified Example)

Channel: sports:scores

- Receiving updates:

```elixir
def join(_, _payload, socket) do

  subscribe(socket, "live_scores")

end
```

Sending updates (triggered by external data source):

Elixir

```elixir
def handle_info({:new_score, score}, socket) do

  broadcast(socket, "live_scores", %{score: score})

end
```

- Updating scores on client-side:

JavaScript

```javascript
// Client-side JavaScript with Phoenix socket

socket.on("live_scores", data => {

  // Update the displayed score using the received data

});
```

These are basic examples, but they illustrate the core concepts: channels, joining, sending/receiving messages, and broadcasting updates. Remember, you can build upon these to create more complex and feature-rich applications.

These are just starting points. You can build more complex chat applications with private messages, user mentions, and emoji reactions. Live feeds can incorporate charts, graphs, and interactive elements for a richer experience.

6.3: Broadcasting Updates and Real-time Collaboration

Imagine your Phoenix application pulsating with life, updates rippling out in real-time, and users collaborating seamlessly. This is the magic of broadcasting and collaboration with Phoenix Channels, empowering you to share information and foster joint action like never before. Let's step into the spotlight and explore!

Broadcasting Updates: Sharing the Spotlight

Think of broadcasting as sending messages to specific groups or the entire world, like an announcer raising their voice to reach everyone. With Phoenix Channels, you have the megaphone in hand, ready to:

- Share breaking news: Send instant updates about major events to all connected users.
- Trigger actions: Notify users about changes in their data, prompting them to react in real-time.
- Coordinate collaborative efforts: Broadcast updates within a specific channel, keeping everyone working on a project synchronized.

Here's the breakdown:

1. Publish and Subscribe: You "publish" messages to a channel, and users can "subscribe" to receive them, filtering the information they see. 2. Push Notifications: Deliver real-time alerts and updates directly to users' browsers, even when they're not actively interacting with your application. 3. Presence: Track who's online and in which channels, facilitating collaboration and targeted communication.

Example (Simplified):

```elixir
defmodule MyApp.NewsChannel do

  use MyApp.Web, :channel

  def handle_info({:breaking_news, headline}, socket) do

    broadcast(socket, "news_updates", %{headline: headline})

  end

end
```

This code shows how to broadcast breaking news headlines to all users subscribed to the news_updates channel.

Collaboration: Sharing the Workspace

Imagine multiple users co-editing a document, crafting together in real-time. Or picture a team brainstorming ideas on a shared whiteboard, instantly seeing each other's contributions. With Phoenix Channels, collaboration becomes a symphony of real-time interaction.

Here's how it works:

- Shared Channels: Dedicate a channel for your collaborative project, like #document_editing or #brainstorming.
- Live Updates: As users make changes, these updates are instantly broadcasted to other participants, keeping everyone on the same page.
- Presence: See who's active in the channel, fostering communication and coordination.

Example (Simplified):

Elixir

```elixir
defmodule MyApp.DocEditorChannel do
```

```elixir
use MyApp.Web, :channel

def handle_in("update_content", %{"content" =>
content}, socket) do

  # Update document content and broadcast the
change

  broadcast(socket, "content_updated", %{content:
content})

  end

end
```

This code demonstrates how users can edit a document collaboratively, with changes broadcasted to everyone in the document_editing channel.

More Examples and code to illustrate Broadcasting Updates with Phoenix Channels:

- Breaking News Alerts:

Elixir

```elixir
defmodule MyApp.NewsChannel do

  use MyApp.Web, :channel
```

```elixir
def handle_info({:breaking_news, headline},
socket) do

  broadcast(socket, "news_updates", %{headline:
headline})

 end

end
```

- Real-time Stock Price Changes:

```elixir
defmodule MyApp.StockAlertsChannel do

 use MyApp.Web, :channel

 def handle_info({:stock_price_change, stock,
price}, socket) do

  user_sockets = get_users_by_stock(stock)

  broadcast(user_sockets, "stock_alert", %{stock:
stock, price: price})

 end

end
```

- Collaborative Project Task Completion:

```elixir
defmodule MyApp.ProjectChannel do

  use MyApp.Web, :channel

  def handle_in("task_completed", %{"task_id" =>
task_id}, socket) do

    broadcast(socket, "task_update", %{task_id:
task_id})

  end

end
```

More simplified examples of Collaboration with Phoenix Channels:

- Live Document Editing:

```elixir
defmodule MyApp.DocEditorChannel do

  use MyApp.Web, :channel
```

```elixir
def handle_in("update_content", %{"content" =>
content}, socket) do

  broadcast(socket, "content_updated", %{content:
content})

  end

end
```

- Shared Whiteboard Drawing:

Elixir

```elixir
defmodule MyApp.WhiteboardChannel do

  use MyApp.Web, :channel

  def handle_in("draw_shape", %{"shape" =>
shape}, socket) do

    broadcast(socket, "shape_drawn", %{shape:
shape})

  end

end
```

These examples showcase the core concepts without unnecessary verbiage. Remember, they're just starting points - you can build upon them to create complex and feature-rich applications!

Broadcasting and collaboration open doors to a world of possibilities. Build real-time auction systems, interactive dashboards, or collaborative games – the potential is limitless.

Chapter 7: APIs and Beyond: RESTful & GraphQL

In this chapter, we'll embark on a thrilling journey, exploring the wonders of RESTful and GraphQL, delving into their strengths, and venturing beyond to discover other exciting API strategies. Buckle up, because we're about to unlock the secrets to seamless data exchange and application integration!

7.1: Building RESTful APIs

At the heart of RESTful APIs lie **resources**, the entities your API manages. Think of them as the actors in your data play – articles, users, products, or any other kind of information you want to expose. To interact with these resources, we use well-defined **CRUD operations**:

- **Create:** Add a new resource, like creating a new user account.
- **Read:** Retrieve existing resources, like fetching a specific article.
- **Update:** Modify existing resources, like updating a product's price.
- **Delete:** Remove resources, like deleting a user's comment.

Each operation maps to a specific **HTTP verb**:

- **GET:** Used to retrieve resources (e.g., GET /articles/123 fetches article with ID 123).
- **POST:** Used to create new resources (e.g., POST /users creates a new user).
- **PUT:** Used to update existing resources (e.g., PUT /products/456 updates product with ID 456).
- **DELETE:** Used to delete resources (e.g., DELETE /comments/789 deletes comment with ID 789).

Think of these verbs as the instructions your API understands, telling it exactly what action to take on the specified resource.

The Language of Data: JSON

How do we exchange data between applications in this grand dance? Enter **JSON**, a lightweight, human-readable format that acts as the common language. Imagine sheet music for the data orchestra, clearly specifying the structure and content of the information being exchanged. This ensures that any application understanding JSON can seamlessly interpret the data sent by your API.

Putting it all Together: A RESTful Example

Let's see a real-world example to solidify these concepts:

```
// Fetch all articles (GET request)

GET /articles

// Create a new user (POST request)

POST /users

{

  "name": "John Doe",

  "email": "john.doe@example.com"

}

// Update an article's title (PUT request)

PUT /articles/123

{

  "title": "A New and Improved Title"

}

// Delete a comment (DELETE request)

DELETE /comments/789
```

In these examples, you can see how HTTP verbs and JSON combine to create clear and concise requests. The API, acting as the conductor, understands these instructions and performs the appropriate CRUD operations on the specified resources.

RESTful APIs offer a well-established, predictable way to structure data exchange. However, it's important to remember that they're not without limitations:

- **Rigidity:** For complex data relationships or scenarios requiring fine-grained control, REST can become cumbersome.
- **Performance:** Large data transfers or nested requests can impact performance due to multiple roundtrips.

While REST remains a dominant force, understanding its strengths and limitations is crucial for making informed decisions about your API architecture.

Here are some code Examples to illustrate these Building Restful APIs:

Resource Interactions:

- Create a new book (POST):

POST /books

Content-Type: application/json

{

 "title": "The Hobbit",

 "author": "J.R.R. Tolkien",

```
  "genre": "Fantasy"

}
```

- Retrieve a specific book by ID (GET):

```
GET /books/123
```

- Update the title of a book (PUT):

```
PUT /books/123

Content-Type: application/json

{

  "title": "The Hobbit: An Unexpected Journey"

}
```

- Delete a book (DELETE):

```
DELETE /books/123
```

- Nested Resources:

```
GET /users/123/comments  // Get all comments of
user with ID 123

POST /articles/456/likes   // Like an article with ID 456
```

PUT /products/789/images/0 // Update the main image of product with ID 789

- Filtering and Sorting:

GET /articles?category=technology&sort=published_at_desc // Get technology articles, sorted by latest first
GET /users?name=john* // Get users whose name starts with "john"

- Error Handling:

JSON

```json
{

  "error": "Not Found",

  "message": "Book with ID 123 not found"

}
```

- Authentication and Authorization:

POST /login

Content-Type: application/json

```json
{

  "username": "alice",

  "password": "secret"
```

```
}
```

// Subsequent requests include an authorization token in the header

GET /users/me

Authorization: Bearer your_token

These are just basic examples. Real-world RESTful APIs can be much more complex with additional features and functionalities.

In the next section, we'll explore a more flexible alternative – GraphQL – and delve into the ever-evolving landscape of API strategies. So, stay tuned, the data exchange symphony continues!

7.2: Integrating GraphQL for Flexible Data Access

In RESTful APIs, clients follow a predefined menu, requesting resources using specific endpoints. But what if they only need a slice of that data? GraphQL flips the script – clients send queries specifying the exact data they require. Think of it as writing a shopping list instead of ordering a full meal.

Here's the key difference:

- **RESTful:** Clients request predefined resources (endpoints).
- **GraphQL:** Clients send queries specifying the desired data structure.

Example (Fetching article title and author name):

GraphQL

```
query {

  article(id: 123) {

    title

    author {

      name

    }

  }

}
```

This query fetches only the **title** and **author.name** from the **article** resource, avoiding unnecessary data transfer and improving efficiency.

Structure and Validation

But how does the API know what data to provide? Enter the **schema** — a blueprint defining the available resources, their properties, and relationships. It acts like a restaurant menu, outlining the available dishes and their ingredients.

- **Types:** Define the structure of data (e.g., Article type with title and author properties).
- **Relationships:** Describe how resources connect (e.g., an Article has one Author).
- **Validation:** Ensures clients request data according to the defined schema.

The schema empowers both clients and the API:

- **Clients:** Understand what data is available and how to request it.
- **API:** Validates queries and provides structured responses.

Benefits of the Flexible Feast: Why Choose GraphQL?

- **Increased Efficiency:** Clients fetch only the data they need, reducing payload size and improving performance.
- **Reduced Complexity:** Complex data relationships are easily queried without multiple roundtrips.

- **Improved Developer Experience:** Clear schema leads to better code predictability and maintainability.

However, it's not a one-size-fits-all solution:

- **Learning Curve:** Understanding the query language and schema design requires additional effort.
- **Complexity for Simple Use Cases:** Overkill for basic data retrieval scenarios.

Putting GraphQL into Action

Here's a basic example showcasing a GraphQL query and response:

- Query:

```GraphQL
query {
 users {
  id
  name
  posts {
   id
```

```
      title
    }
  }
}
```

- Response:

JSON

```json
{
  "data": {
    "users": [
      {
        "id": 1,
        "name": "Alice",
        "posts": [
          {
            "id": 2,
            "title": "My First Post"
          },
          {
```

```
      "id": 3,

      "title": "Another Great Post"

    }

  ]

 },

  // ... other users

 ]

 }

}
```

GraphQL offers a powerful alternative to RESTful APIs, especially for complex data interactions and client-driven data needs. As you explore its potential, consider its trade-offs to make informed decisions for your API architecture.

In the next section, we'll explore other exciting API strategies beyond RESTful and GraphQL, expanding your horizons in the ever-evolving landscape of data exchange!

7.3: Exploring Other API Strategies

The API landscape is a vibrant dance floor, not limited to just the graceful waltz of REST and the freestyle flow of GraphQL. Let's loosen up and explore some other captivating rhythms that might suit your API needs!

Stepping into the High-Performance Zone with gRPC:

Imagine two dancers moving in perfect synchronicity, exchanging information seamlessly. That's the essence of gRPC, a high-performance protocol built for speed and efficiency. Here's what makes it special:

- **Binary Format:** Data is exchanged in a compact binary format, reducing payload size and boosting performance, especially for large datasets or frequent communication.
- **Streaming:** Enables continuous data flow between applications, ideal for real-time scenarios like video streaming or live data feeds.
- **Strong Typing:** Enforces strict data structures, ensuring data integrity and reducing errors.

Example (gRPC for stock price updates):

// Client-side code (gRPC library)

const stockService = new StockService();

```
const updates = stockService.GetLivePrices(["AAPL",
"GOOG"]);

updates.onData((data) => {

 // Update UI with latest stock prices

});

// Server-side code (gRPC server)

const prices = GetStockPrices(["AAPL", "GOOG"]);

stream.write(prices[0]);

stream.write(prices[1]);
```

While powerful, gRPC has a steeper learning curve and might be overkill for simple use cases.

Embracing Real-Time with WebSockets:

Imagine dancers responding to each other's movements instantly, creating a dynamic flow. That's the power of WebSockets, a technology enabling real-time, two-way communication between applications.

- **Persistent Connection:** Unlike HTTP requests, WebSockets establish a long-lived connection, allowing for continuous data exchange without roundtrips.

- **Push-based Updates:** Servers can proactively send data to clients as it becomes available, ideal for live notifications or chat applications.

Example (WebSocket for chat messages):

JavaScript

```javascript
// Client-side code (using a WebSocket library)

const socket = new
WebSocket("ws://localhost:8080/chat");

socket.onmessage = (event) => {

  // Display received message

};

// Server-side code (WebSocket server)

const clients = []; // List of connected clients

const message = "New message!";

clients.forEach((client) => client.send(message));
```

WebSockets are best suited for scenarios requiring constant data updates, not occasional data fetching.

Going Serverless for Scalability and Agility:

Imagine a dance troupe where each dancer focuses on their part, seamlessly adapting to the music's changes. That's the serverless approach, where APIs leverage cloud infrastructure to handle requests dynamically.

- **Event-driven**: APIs respond to events triggered by data changes or user actions, promoting scalability and flexibility.
- **Pay-per-use**: You only pay for the resources used, optimizing costs and eliminating server management overhead.

Example (Serverless function for image resizing):

JavaScript

```javascript
exports.resizeImage = async (event) => {

  const imageData = event.data;

  const resizedImage = resize(imageData);

  return resizedImage;

};
```

While serverless offers scalability and cost benefits, it might introduce vendor lock-in and require careful consideration of event-driven architecture.

The perfect API strategy depends on your specific needs and priorities. Consider factors like performance, complexity, real-time requirements, and scalability when making your choice. So, keep exploring, experiment, and find the rhythm that makes your API data dance to the beat of your application's success!

Chapter 8: Unlocking Performance: Concurrency and Optimization

---

In this chapter, we'll delve into the world of **concurrency** and **optimization**, learning how to make your applications dance like a well-rehearsed orchestra, handling data with speed and efficiency. Buckle up, because we're about to explore Elixir's unique concurrency model and unleash the full potential of your applications!

8.1: Elixir's Concurrency Model - Processes and GenServers

The essence of Elixir's concurrency model – a powerful dance of **processes** and **GenServers**, working in concert to achieve remarkable performance and scalability. Let's break down the key players and how they create this magic.

Processes

Unlike traditional threads, Elixir relies on **lightweight processes** – independent actors that act as the workhorses of your application. Think of them as individual vendors in the marketplace, each handling their own tasks concurrently. They communicate with each other through **message passing**, ensuring clear and isolated interactions.

Benefits of Processes:

- **Scalability:** Easily handle high volumes of concurrent requests without performance bottlenecks.
- **Fault Tolerance:** Individual processes are isolated, so one failing vendor doesn't bring down the entire market (application).
- **Maintainability:** Code is modular and easier to understand and debug, like analyzing specific vendor interactions.

Example: Imagine an e-commerce application processing several orders simultaneously. Each order can be handled by a separate process, independently calculating discounts, updating inventory, and generating invoices.

GenServers

But how do these processes coordinate and share information efficiently? Enter the **GenServer** − a special process designed for structured communication and state management. Think of it as the market's central hub, responsible for routing messages between vendors and ensuring everyone has the latest information.

Key Features of GenServers:

- **State Management:** GenServers can store and manage data, acting as a central information repository for related processes.
- **Structured Communication:** They define clear interfaces for processes to interact, ensuring well-defined message exchange.
- **Supervision:** GenServers can supervise other processes, automatically restarting them in case of failures, contributing to robustness.

Example: In our e-commerce application, a GenServer might manage the product catalog, receiving messages from processes to fetch product details and update inventory when orders are placed.

Processes and GenServers in Action

The true magic happens when processes and GenServers work together. Processes leverage GenServers for coordinated communication and data access, creating a scalable and resilient system. This collaboration is what empowers Elixir applications to handle complex workloads efficiently and gracefully.

Here are some concrete examples and code to understand them better.

Processes in Action

Example 1: Processing multiple web requests concurrently

```elixir
def handle_request(conn, request) do

  # Create a separate process for each request

  spawn fn ->

   process_request(conn, request)

  end

  # Continue handling other requests while the spawned process works

  send_response(conn, 202, "Processing")

end

def process_request(conn, request) do

  # Simulate some work

  Process.sleep(1000)

  # Respond with the processed data

  send_response(conn, 200, "Data processed!")

end
```

This code demonstrates how multiple web requests can be handled concurrently using processes. Each request spawns a separate process, allowing the server to serve other requests while the previous ones are being processed.

Example 2: Background tasks with processes

```elixir
Elixir

def send_welcome_email(user) do

  spawn fn ->

    Email.send("welcome@example.com", user.email, "Welcome to our platform!")

  end

end
```

Here, we spawn a process to send a welcome email in the background, allowing the main process to continue with other tasks without waiting for the email to be sent.

GenServers in Action

Example 1: Managing a shopping cart with a GenServer

```elixir
Elixir

defmodule Cart do
```

```
use GenServer

def start_link(_) do

  GenServer.start_link(__MODULE__, [], [])

end

def add_item(pid, item) do

  GenServer.cast(pid, {:add_item, item})

end

def get_items(pid) do

  GenServer.call(pid, :get_items)

end

  # ... implementation details for handling messages
and state ...

end
```

This GenServer manages a shopping cart's state, allowing processes to add and retrieve items without directly accessing shared data. This ensures data consistency and avoids potential concurrency issues.

Example 2: Supervising child processes with a GenServer

```elixir
defmodule WorkerSupervisor do

  use Supervisor

  def start_link(_) do

    Supervisor.start_link(__MODULE__, [], [])

  end

  def init(_) do

    children = [

      worker(Worker, [])

    ]

    Supervisor.start_link(children, restart: :transient)

  end

  # ... implementation for handling child process supervision ...

end
```

This GenServer supervises worker processes, restarting them automatically in case of failures, contributing to the overall robustness of the system.

Understanding this foundation is crucial for building high-performing Elixir applications. So, don't hesitate to experiment, explore different processes and GenServer scenarios, and watch your applications dance with data like a perfectly synchronized orchestra!

In the next section, we'll delve deeper into optimizing your applications further, unlocking their full potential for scalability and performance. Stay tuned!

8.2: Optimizing Application Performance for Scalability

The first step to optimization is **identifying bottlenecks**. Imagine traffic slowing down at a specific junction. We need to pinpoint the cause – is it a broken traffic light, an accident, or simply high volume? Similarly, profiling tools like **cProfile** or **iex-prof** help you identify areas in your code that are slowing things down.

Example: Profiling reveals a function responsible for complex data processing is taking excessive time. This becomes your target for optimization.

Streamlining the Flow:

Imagine cars waiting unnecessarily at a green light. Lazy evaluation avoids such preemptive work. It delays computations until they are absolutely required, optimizing resource usage. Libraries like Stream and Enum offer powerful tools for lazy evaluation.

Example: Instead of loading an entire dataset into memory at once, process it chunk by chunk using Stream.chunk, reducing memory pressure and improving performance.

Pattern Matching Prowess

Pattern matching in Elixir empowers you with similar precision for data manipulation. By extracting specific data patterns efficiently, you can streamline operations.

Example: Instead of using multiple if statements, leverage pattern matching to concisely extract different fields from complex data structures, enhancing code readability and performance.

Stream Processing for Big Data

Stream processing handles large datasets similarly. By processing data in manageable chunks, you avoid overwhelming your system and ensure smooth operation.

Example: Process sensor data from thousands of devices in real-time using libraries like GenStage or Flywheel, breaking down the data into smaller, manageable streams for efficient analysis.

Caching: The Strategic Reserve for Speedy Retrieval

Caching works similarly, storing frequently accessed data in memory for faster retrieval, reducing database load and improving response times.

Example: Cache frequently accessed product information in your e-commerce application to avoid database queries for every user request, leading to faster product page loading times.

Let's explore optimization techniques with concrete examples and code to transform your app into a performance champion!

- Unveiling Bottlenecks: The Power of Profiling

Concept: Identify performance bottlenecks using profiling tools like cProfile or iex-prof.

Example:

```bash
Bash

# Profile a function using cProfile
```

cprofile -o profile.out my_function

Analyze the **profile.out** file to pinpoint functions consuming excessive time.

- Streamlining the Flow

Concept: Delay computations until absolutely necessary with libraries like **Stream** and **Enum**.

Example:

```elixir
Elixir
defmodule LargeDataset do
  def process(data) do
    data
    |> Stream.chunk(100)
    |> Enum.map(&expensive_computation/1)
  end
end
```

This processes a large dataset in chunks, avoiding loading everything in memory at once.

- Pattern Matching Prowess

Concept: Use pattern matching for efficient data manipulation and extraction.

Example:

```elixir
Elixir

def handle_request(conn, %{path: "/users/:id"}) do

  # Extract user ID directly from the path

  get_user(id) |> render(conn)

end
```

This avoids using multiple **if** statements to extract the user ID from the request path.

- Stream Processing for Big Data

Concept: Process large datasets in manageable chunks with libraries like **GenStage** or **Flywheel**.

Example:

```elixir
Elixir

defmodule SensorDataProcessor do

  use GenStage

  def handle_cast({:data, data_chunk}) do
```

```
  process_data(data_chunk)

 end

end
```

This GenStage processes sensor data chunks received as messages, avoiding overwhelming the system.

- Caching: The Strategic Reserve for Speedy Retrieval

Concept: Store frequently accessed data in memory for faster retrieval using libraries like Cachex.

Example:

```Elixir
def get_product(id) do

 Cachex.get(:products, id) || fetch_product(id) |>
Cachex.put(:products, id)

end
```

This caches product information, reducing database load for frequently accessed products.

By understanding these optimization techniques and applying them diligently, you can transform your Elixir application into a well-oiled machine, handling traffic with grace and efficiency. So, buckle up, embrace the spirit of experimentation, and optimize your way to application performance excellence!

8.3: Monitoring and Debugging Techniques

Let's explore techniques to identify and address issues before they disrupt the performance.

Unveiling the Secrets: The Power of Logging

Think of logging as leaving notes for yourself and future collaborators. Logs record events and messages within your application, providing valuable insights into its behavior. Libraries like Logger and Phoenix.Logger offer powerful logging capabilities.

Example: Log user login attempts and successful transactions to monitor application activity and identify potential security concerns.

Metrics Galore:

Application metrics provide similar insights, quantifying key performance indicators (KPIs) like request processing times, memory usage, and database connections. Tools like Telex and Prometheus capture and visualize these metrics.

Example: Track response times for critical API endpoints to identify performance bottlenecks and ensure they stay within acceptable ranges.

Testing:

Imagine rehearsing a musical piece before the grand performance. Testing plays a similar role, ensuring your application behaves as expected and catching issues early. Unit tests verify individual functions, while integration tests assess how components interact. Tools like ExUnit and Bamboo support comprehensive testing strategies.

Example: Write unit tests for your data processing functions to guarantee they produce accurate results under various input scenarios.

Debugging:

Imagine the conductor diagnosing a wrong note and guiding the musician to play correctly. Debuggers like iex and breakpoint allow you to step through your code line by line, inspecting variables and identifying the source of errors.

Example: Use iex to debug an unexpected error in your user registration process, pinpointing the exact line of code causing the issue.

Let's explore these techniques with concrete examples and code to keep your app in top shape!

- Unveiling the Secrets: The Power of Logging

Concept: Record events and messages within your application for later analysis.

Example:

```elixir
Elixir

defmodule MyApp do

  use Phoenix.Endpoint

  plug Logger

  def handle_call(_, state) do

    Logger.info("Processing request for #{state.user_id}")

    # ... process request ...

  end

end
```

This logs information about user ID when processing a request, aiding in tracking user activity and potential issues.

- Metrics Galore:

Concept: Capture and visualize key performance indicators (KPIs) like response times and memory usage.

Example:

```elixir
Elixir

defmodule MyApp do

  use Phoenix.Endpoint

  plug Telemetry, metrics: [:response_time, :memory]

end
```

This plugs the Telemetry middleware to automatically collect response time and memory usage metrics, which can be visualized in tools like Grafana for analysis.

- Testing:

Concept: Write unit and integration tests to ensure code behaves as expected and catch issues early.

Example (Unit test):

Elixir

```elixir
test "calculate_discount/2 returns correct discount" do

  assert MyApp.calculate_discount(100, 10) == 90

end
```

This unit test verifies the **calculate_discount** function produces the correct result.

Example (Integration test):

Elixir

```elixir
test "user_registration_flow creates a user" do

  # Simulate user registration flow and assert user is created in the database

end
```

This integration test ensures the entire user registration process functions correctly.

- Debugging:

Concept: Step through your code line by line to identify the source of errors.

Example:

```
iex -I mix

iex> MyApp.get_user(1) # This raises an error

iex> c = :erlang.whereis(:gen_server_1) # Inspect the GenServer process

iex> GenServer.call(c, {:info, []}) # Get process information for debugging
```

Here, we use **iex** to debug an error in **get_user**, inspecting the GenServer process involved to pinpoint the issue.

These techniques work best when combined. Logs provide context for metrics, metrics guide testing efforts, and tests aid in effective debugging. By using them together, you can proactively maintain your Elixir application's health and deliver an exceptional user experience.

Chapter 9: Building Scalable and Distributed Systems

In this chapter, we'll embark on a captivating journey, exploring how Elixir empowers you to build such scalable and resilient systems.

9.1: Introduction to Distributed Systems with Elixir

In this section, we'll delve into the exciting world of distributed systems built with Elixir, empowering you to create scalable and resilient applications.

Why Go Distributed? Understanding the Benefits

Think of a restaurant struggling to keep up with peak hour demand. Adding more tables in the same space might not be the answer. Distributed systems offer similar solutions for software:

- **Scalability:** Easily handle increased workloads by distributing tasks across multiple servers, just like adding more restaurants across the city to serve more customers.

- **High Availability:** No single point of failure – if one server encounters an issue, others can continue operations, ensuring your application remains accessible, like having backup restaurants open during emergencies.
- **Geographic Distribution:** Serve users globally by strategically placing servers in different regions, reducing latency and improving user experience, just like having restaurants closer to different customer segments.

Elixir's Toolkit for Building Distributed Dreams

Elixir provides powerful tools to turn your distributed system dreams into reality:

- **OTP Framework:** The foundation, offering robust building blocks for fault tolerance and distribution, like having a reliable infrastructure to build your restaurants upon.
- **GenServers:** Lightweight processes ideal for managing concurrent tasks across servers, like chefs handling individual orders simultaneously in different restaurants.
- **Clustering Mechanisms:** Tools like Phoenix Clustering and GenServer clustering enable seamless coordination between multiple servers, ensuring smooth communication and

collaboration between your geographically distributed restaurants.

Example: Imagine an e-commerce application with separate servers handling product searches, order processing, and payments. Distributed systems ensure each function operates efficiently, even if one server experiences high load.

Key Considerations for Distributed Systems

Building a distributed system is like managing a multi-restaurant chain – careful planning and coordination are crucial:

- **Complexity:** Distributed systems introduce additional complexity compared to single-server setups. Consider the trade-offs carefully before diving in.
- **Network Communication:** Efficient communication between servers is essential, like having a reliable delivery network between your restaurants.
- **Data Consistency:** Maintaining consistent data across multiple servers can be challenging. Explore strategies like distributed databases or eventual consistency models.

Remember, the decision to go distributed depends on your specific needs and requirements. But when used effectively, Elixir empowers you to build applications that scale gracefully and remain resilient, just like a well-coordinated restaurant chain delighting customers worldwide.

This introduction equips you with a foundational understanding of distributed systems and Elixir's capabilities. In the next section, we'll delve deeper into specific cluster management techniques and fault tolerance strategies, helping you build even more robust and scalable applications.

9.2: Cluster Management and Supervision Trees

Imagine an orchestra, not confined to a single stage, but its sections spread across various halls, playing in perfect harmony. Cluster management and supervision trees in Elixir empower you to achieve this in your distributed systems, ensuring seamless coordination and resilience across multiple servers. Let's delve into this fascinating world!

Cluster Management Tools

Think of a conductor meticulously coordinating different sections of the orchestra. Cluster management tools in Elixir serve a similar purpose for your distributed system:

- **Phoenix Clustering:** Manages a group of Phoenix servers, ensuring they run the same code and handle requests efficiently. Imagine different orchestra halls using synchronized sheet music and conductors.
- **GenServer Clustering:** Distributes GenServers across multiple servers, ensuring fault tolerance and scalability for long-running processes. Picture individual musicians in different locations, each playing their part in the overall symphony.

Benefits of Cluster Management:

- **High Availability:** If one server encounters an issue, others can take over, ensuring your application remains operational. Imagine the music continuing even if one instrument malfunctions.
- **Load Balancing:** Distributes requests evenly across servers, preventing performance bottlenecks. Think of the conductor strategically assigning difficult passages to different sections for a balanced performance.
- **Simplified Deployment:** Manage and update your application across multiple servers from a single point. Imagine easily changing the sheet music for all orchestra halls simultaneously.

Building a Resilient System: Supervision Trees

Now, imagine each musician in the orchestra having an understudy ready to jump in if needed. Supervision trees in Elixir provide similar functionality:

- Define how processes are linked and restarted in case of failures, forming a resilient structure for your distributed system. Picture a chain of command ensuring someone can always cover for an absent musician.
- Allow for granular control over process restarts, preventing cascading failures. Imagine restarting only the specific instrument section encountering issues, not the entire orchestra.

Example: Implement a supervision tree for your e-commerce application, ensuring critical processes like order processing automatically restart if they encounter errors. This prevents a single issue from bringing down the entire system.

Putting It All Together: A Distributed Masterpiece

Building a robust distributed system requires combining these tools effectively:

- **Cluster management** ensures servers work together seamlessly.
- **Supervision trees** guarantee individual processes are resilient.

- **Monitoring and logging** provide insights into system health.

Remember, the optimal approach depends on your specific needs and complexity. Experiment, explore different tools and strategies, and continuously monitor your system's performance and resilience.

Here are some code Examples to illustrate Cluster Management and Supervision Trees :

Cluster Management:

- Phoenix Clustering:

```Elixir
defmodule MyApp.Endpoint do

  use Phoenix.Endpoint, cluster: MyApp.ClusterConfig

end
```

- GenServer Clustering:

```Elixir
defmodule MyApp.Worker do

  use GenServer

  # ... worker logic ...

end
```

```
GenServer.start_link(MyApp.Worker, [], [])
```

Supervision Trees:

```elixir
defmodule MyApp.Supervisor do

  use Supervisor

  def start_link(args) do

    Supervisor.start_link(__MODULE__, :ok,
children: [

      worker: {MyApp.Worker, [], restart: :transient},

      # ... other child processes ...

    ])
  end
end
```

Combining both:

```elixir
defmodule MyApp.App do

  use Application
```

```elixir
def start(_type, _args) do

  # Start Phoenix endpoint with clustering

  MyApp.Endpoint.start(cluster:
MyApp.ClusterConfig)

  # Define supervision tree with child processes

  Supervisor.start_link(MyApp.Supervisor, :ok, [])

  # Start monitoring and logging

  Telemetry.start_metrics(:my_app)

 end

end
```

Remember, these are just basic examples. The specific implementation will vary depending on your application's needs.

By mastering these concepts, you can create Elixir applications that scale gracefully, handle failures elegantly, and deliver a consistently exceptional experience, just like a perfectly synchronized distributed orchestra captivating its audience.

In the next section, we'll delve deeper into specific fault tolerance strategies, empowering you to build even more robust and reliable distributed systems.

9.3: Fault Tolerance and High Availability Strategies

Think of fault tolerance as building a sturdy marketplace with backup generators and rain-proof stalls. It ensures your application keeps functioning even when individual components fail. High availability is like having multiple marketplaces across town, guaranteeing service remains accessible even if one location closes. Let's explore these key strategies in detail:

1. Redundancy:

- Duplicate critical services and data on multiple servers, ensuring no single point of failure. Imagine having multiple vendors selling the same products, so customers can still find what they need even if one stall closes.

Elixir

```elixir
defmodule MyApp.Database do

  use MyApp.Cluster

  def get_user(id) do

    # Access user data from any available database server

  end
```

end

2. Automatic Failover:

- Configure automatic switching to backup servers when failures occur. Think of having backup generators automatically powering the marketplace when the main power goes out.

Elixir

```elixir
defmodule MyApp.GenServer do

  use GenServer

  def init(_) do

    {:ok, %{primary_server: :server1,
    secondary_server: :server2}}

  end

  def handle_cast({:failover}, state) do

    {:noreply, %{state | primary_server:
    state.secondary_server}}

  end
end
```

3. Circuit Breakers:

- Protect downstream services from cascading failures by temporarily pausing requests under heavy load. Imagine closing access to specific stalls during peak hours to prevent overcrowding in the entire marketplace.

Elixir

```elixir
defmodule MyApp.RateLimiter do

  use GenServer

  def start_link(_) do

    GenServer.start_link(__MODULE__, :ok, [])

  end

  def allow_request? do

    # Check if request rate exceeds limit and return true/false

  end

end
```

4. Supervision Trees:

- Define how processes are linked and restarted in case of failures, forming a resilient structure.

Imagine each stall having an understudy vendor ready to step in if needed.

```elixir
defmodule MyApp.Supervisor do

  use Supervisor

  def start_link(args) do

    Supervisor.start_link(__MODULE__, :ok, children: [

      worker: {MyApp.Worker, [], restart: :transient},

      # ... other child processes ...

    ])

  end

end
```

Choosing the Right Strategy: It's All About Context

The best strategy depends on your specific needs and application requirements. Consider factors like:

- **Criticality of service:** How crucial is continuous operation?
- **Expected failure rate:** How often do you anticipate issues?

- **Cost and complexity**: Are complex redundancy setups feasible?

By mastering these concepts, you can build Elixir applications that weather any storm, just like a well-prepared marketplace adapting to any challenge and continuing to serve its customers with exceptional experiences.

In the next chapter, we'll delve deeper into specific distributed system architectures and communication patterns, empowering you to build even more sophisticated and resilient applications.

Chapter 10: Advanced Phoenix Features and Security

Imagine a master chef, able to whip up culinary masterpieces while simultaneously tweaking ingredients and perfecting techniques. That's the power you unlock with advanced Phoenix features, enhancing your development efficiency and crafting secure, robust applications. Buckle up for a delicious exploration of hot reloading, code generation, testing strategies, and security best practices!

10.1 Hot Reloading and Code Generation for Efficiency

The magic of hot reloading and code generation in Phoenix – empowering you to sculpt your Elixir applications with unparalleled speed and efficiency. Let's delve into these productivity boosters, equipping you to streamline your development workflow!

Hot Reloading - Instant Feedback, Agile Development

Ever spend precious minutes restarting your server after making a tiny code change? Hot reloading eliminates that pain, letting you see changes reflected in your browser **instantly**. It's like having a live preview of your sculpting, allowing you to iterate rapidly and fine-tune your application with ease.

Key Features:

- **LiveReload:** Witness code changes, like variable updates or function modifications, reflected in your browser almost immediately. Imagine adding a touch of color to your sculpture and seeing it come alive instantly.
- **HotCode:** Modify Phoenix views and templates on the fly, observing the visual updates in your browser without a server restart. It's like shaping the finer details of your sculpture in real-time.

Benefits:

- **Faster development:** Iterate quickly, experiment freely, and identify issues sooner, saving you valuable time.
- **Improved feedback loop:** See the impact of your changes instantly, leading to more focused and efficient development.
- **Enhanced developer experience:** Enjoy a smooth and dynamic coding experience, keeping you engaged and productive.

Example:

1. Implement a new styling rule in your CSS file.

2. With LiveReload active, watch the changes applied to your web page **without** refreshing.
3. Adjust the rule values and see the visual updates instantly, refining your design with ease.

Code Generation - Automation for Repetitive Tasks

Imagine having an assistant who tirelessly handles the mundane tasks, freeing you to focus on the creative aspects. Phoenix code generation acts as your Elixir assistant, automatically creating boilerplate code for common tasks:

- **Generators:** Craft essential components like controllers, views, and models with a single command. Think of it as having pre-made clay templates for different sculpture parts, saving you time shaping them from scratch.
- **Custom generators:** Tailor generators to your specific needs, creating unique templates for frequently used components. Imagine designing your own custom clay molds for specialized sculpture elements.

Benefits:

- **Reduced boilerplate:** Spend less time writing repetitive code and more time on application logic.

- **Consistency:** Ensure consistent code structure and naming conventions throughout your project.
- **Faster development:** Get started on new features more quickly, focusing on the unique aspects of your application.

Example:

1. Run `phoenix generate User` to create a model, controller, and views for managing users, saving you time writing repetitive CRUD code.
2. Customize the generated files to add specific functionalities relevant to your user model.

Remember: While code generation saves time, it's crucial to understand the generated code and modify it as needed to fit your application's specific requirements.

Examples and code to illustrate Hot Reloading and Code Generation

- Hot Reloading:

LiveReload:

1. Modify a variable value in your Elixir code.

2. Observe the change reflected in your browser instantly (requires LiveReload integration).

HotCode:

1. Update a CSS style rule in your app.css file.
2. Witness the visual changes applied to your web page without refreshing.
   - Code Generation:

Phoenix Generator:

```Bash
phoenix generate User
```

This creates a complete set of files including:

- lib/your_app/models/user.ex (model definition)
- lib/your_app/controllers/user_controller.ex (controller logic)
- lib/your_app/views/user/index.html.eex (list view)
- lib/your_app/views/user/show.html.eex (show view)
- lib/your_app/views/user/new.html.eex (new form)
- lib/your_app/views/user/edit.html.eex (edit form)

Custom Generator:

Create a custom generator for "Article" entities:

Elixir

```elixir
defmodule YourApp.ArticleGenerator do

  use Phoenix.Generator

  def generate(name, options) do

    # Generate custom code for your Article model,
    controller, and views

  end

end
```

Run the generator:

Bash

```bash
mix phoenix.gen.your_app.article Article
```

Remember, these are just basic examples. The specific implementation will vary depending on your project's needs.

By harnessing the power of hot reloading and code generation, you can streamline your development process, iterate faster, and focus on crafting exceptional Elixir applications with agility and efficiency. Remember, these tools are there to empower you, not replace your understanding of the underlying code.

10.2 Testing Strategies: Unit and Integration Testing

Imagine a master architect meticulously testing each brick before constructing a majestic castle. That's the essence of testing in Elixir – ensuring the individual components and their interactions function flawlessly, leading to a robust and reliable application. Let's explore two fundamental testing strategies: unit testing and integration testing, equipping you to build applications with confidence!

Unit Testing

Think of unit testing as examining each brick individually, ensuring it meets specific quality standards. In Elixir, unit tests focus on isolating and testing individual functions and modules:

- **Mock dependencies:** Simulate external dependencies like databases to test your code in

isolation, like examining the structural integrity of a brick without relying on the entire wall.
- **Assert expected behavior:** Write clear assertions to verify that your function outputs match the desired results, like confirming a brick meets specific strength and size requirements.

Benefits:

- **Early bug detection:** Identify issues early in the development process, preventing them from cascading into larger problems.
- **Improved code quality:** Tests act as documentation and safety nets, encouraging clean and maintainable code.
- **Faster development:** Refactor and modify code with confidence, knowing existing functionality remains intact.

Example:

Elixir

```
def test "add function returns correct sum" do

  assert 5 == MyMath.add(2, 3)

end
```

This test checks if the **add** function in the **MyMath** module returns the expected sum for the given inputs.

Integration Testing

Now, imagine testing how the bricks work together to form a sturdy wall. Integration testing focuses on verifying interactions between different components of your application:

- **Test multiple components:** Simulate how your model interacts with your controller and views, like ensuring bricks fit together seamlessly to form a strong wall section.
- **Focus on data flow:** Verify that data is passed correctly between components and processed as expected, like checking if mortar binds the bricks together effectively.

Benefits:

- **Increased confidence in system behavior:** Ensure your application functions as a whole, not just individual components.
- **Reduced risk of regressions:** Identify integration issues before they impact users.
- **Improved system understanding:** Gain deeper insight into how different parts of your application work together.

Example:

```Elixir
```

```
def test "create user action saves user and redirects"
do

  # Simulate user input, call controller action, and test
database changes and redirection.

end
```

This test verifies that the create user action in your controller correctly saves user data, redirects to the appropriate page, and interacts with the database as expected.

Building a Testing Fortress: Combining Strategies

Remember, both unit and integration testing are crucial for building a secure and reliable application. Use them strategically:

- **Start with unit tests:** Test individual components thoroughly before integrating them.
- **Complement with integration tests:** Verify how components interact and ensure overall system behavior.
- **Test at different levels:** Combine unit and integration tests for comprehensive coverage.

Examples & Codes to illustrate the concepts:

Unit Testing:

- Testing a sum function:

Elixir

```elixir
def test "sum function adds numbers correctly" do
  assert 10 == MyMath.sum(5, 5)
  assert -3 == MyMath.sum(-2, -1)
end
```

- Testing a model validation:

Elixir

```elixir
def test "user model validates presence of name" do
  user = %User{email: "test@example.com"}
  assert {:error, [{:name, :blank}]} ==
User.validate(user)
end
```

Integration Testing:

- Testing user creation:

Elixir

```elixir
def test "create user action saves user and redirects"
do
  # Simulate user input (e.g., via a post request)
```

Call the controller action responsible for creating the user

  # Assert that the user is saved in the database

  # Assert that the user is redirected to the appropriate page

end

- Testing product purchase flow:

Elixir

```elixir
def test "adding product to cart and checking out completes purchase" do
  # Simulate adding a product to the cart
  # Simulate checkout process
  # Assert that the order is created in the database
  # Assert that payment is processed successfully
end
```

These are just basic examples. The specific tests will vary depending on your application's functionality and complexity.

By adopting these testing strategies, you'll build Elixir applications with confidence, knowing each brick is strong and the overall structure is sound, ready to withstand any challenges.

In the next section, we'll explore security best practices to fortify your Elixir applications, ensuring they are not only functional but also resistant to potential vulnerabilities.

10.3: Security Best Practices and Common Vulnerabilities

Imagine a majestic castle, not just grand but also meticulously fortified against invaders. That's the essence of security in Elixir applications – proactively safeguarding your users' data and ensuring the integrity of your system. Let's delve into essential security best practices and common vulnerabilities, empowering you to build applications that are both powerful and secure!

Understanding the Threats: Common Vulnerabilities

Think of vulnerabilities as weaknesses in your castle walls that attackers can exploit. Here are some common ones in Elixir applications:

- **Cross-Site Scripting (XSS):** Malicious scripts injected into your application can harm users. Imagine an attacker sneaking a hidden weapon past your guards.
- **SQL Injection:** Untrusted user input can manipulate database queries, potentially compromising sensitive data. Picture an attacker using a battering ram disguised as a gift to breach your armory.
- **Cross-Site Request Forgery (CSRF):** Attackers can trick users into performing unauthorized actions. Imagine an enemy manipulating your guards to open the gates for their allies.

Security Best Practices

Now, let's equip your castle with robust defenses:

- **Input Validation:** Sanitize user input to prevent malicious code injection, like inspecting all incoming visitors and confiscating any suspicious items.
- **Authorization:** Control user access to specific resources based on their roles and permissions, like granting access to different castle areas only to authorized personnel.
- **Encryption:** Secure sensitive data like passwords and credit card information, like storing valuables in a heavily guarded vault.

Additional Best Practices:

- **Stay updated:** Regularly patch your dependencies and libraries to address known vulnerabilities, like keeping your castle defenses up-to-date with the latest technology.
- **Follow security guidelines:** Adhere to established security frameworks like OWASP to minimize risks, like following proven defense strategies recommended by experienced guards.
- **Perform security audits:** Conduct regular security assessments to identify and address potential weaknesses, like inviting security experts to inspect your castle for vulnerabilities.

Remember, security is an ongoing process, not a one-time fix. By diligently following these best practices and staying vigilant, you can build Elixir applications that are secure and trustworthy, offering a safe haven for your users.

Here are more Illustrative Examples & Code for Security Best Practices and Common Vulnerabilities

Security best practices

- Input Validation:

Elixir

```
defmodule MyApp.UserController do
```

```elixir
def create(conn, params) do

  cleaned_params = %{

    name: String.trim(params["name"]),

    email: Ecto.Changeset.cast(params, %User{},
[:email], &String.trim/1)

  }

  # ... further processing ...

 end
end
```

- Authorization:

```elixir
defmodule MyApp.PostController do

 def index(conn, _params) do

  current_user = Guardian.Plug.current_user(conn)

  if current_user do

   posts = Repo.all(Post)

   render(conn, "index.html", posts: posts)

  else
```

```elixir
    conn |> put_flash(:error, "You must be logged in
to access posts")

    |> redirect(to: "/")

  end

 end

end
```

- Encryption:

Elixir

```elixir
defmodule MyApp.UserController do

 def create(conn, params) do

  user = %{

   name: params["name"],

   password:
Comeonin.Bcrypt.hashpwsalt(params["password"])

  }

  Repo.insert!(user)

  # ... further processing ...

 end
```

end

Common Vulnerabilities:

- XSS:

```Elixir
# Vulnerable code (don't use!)
def render_comment(conn, comment) do
  raw "<p>#{comment}</p>"
end
```

- SQL Injection:

```Elixir
# Vulnerable code (don't use!)
def search_users(name) do
  query = "SELECT * FROM users WHERE name = '#{name}'"
  Repo.query(query)
end
```

- CSRF:

```HTML
```

Vulnerable form (don't use!)

```
<form action="/transfer" method="post">

  <input type="hidden" name="_csrf_token" value="secret_token">

  <input type="number" name="amount">

  <button type="submit">Transfer</button>

</form>
```

These are just basic examples. The specific implementation will vary depending on your application's needs and complexity. Always consult best practices and security guidelines for your specific use case.

By understanding common vulnerabilities and adopting these security best practices, you can build Elixir applications that are not only powerful but also safe and secure, standing strong like an impregnable castle protecting its treasures.

Bonus Chapter: Real-world Case Studies and Applications

Elixir isn't just a language for academics – it's a powerful tool used by real companies to build robust, scalable applications. Let's embark on a journey through diverse case studies, witnessing how Elixir empowers businesses across industries:

1. WhatsApp: Scaling Communication with Elixir

Imagine billions of messages zipping around the globe seamlessly – that's the magic of WhatsApp, and Elixir plays a crucial role. Its concurrency features and fault tolerance enable WhatsApp to handle massive message volumes effortlessly, ensuring smooth communication for millions.

Key Learnings:

- Elixir's scalability and fault tolerance are perfect for high-traffic applications.
- OTP framework provides robust messaging and supervision capabilities.

2. Pinterest: Building a Visually Engaging Platform with Elixir

Picture millions of images and pins being served efficiently – that's Pinterest, leveraging Elixir's pattern matching and hot reloading for a dynamic user experience.

Key Learnings:

- Elixir's pattern matching simplifies complex data manipulation for image processing.
- Hot reloading facilitates rapid feature development and iteration.

3. Discord: Creating a Real-time Chat Experience with Elixir

Imagine real-time chat with minimal latency – that's Discord, utilizing Elixir's GenServers and Phoenix Channels for efficient communication and collaboration.

Key Learnings:

- GenServers enable efficient actor concurrency for handling multiple chat sessions.
- Phoenix Channels facilitate real-time communication with low latency.

4. Bleacher Report: Delivering Sports News with Elixir's Speed

Think about delivering up-to-the-minute sports news instantly – that's Bleacher Report, relying on Elixir's speed and concurrency to keep fans informed.

Key Learnings:

- Elixir's speed and concurrency ensure fast data processing and content delivery.
- OTP framework provides robust error handling and supervision for reliable operation.

5. Heroku: Building a Cloud Platform with Elixir's Scalability

Imagine managing millions of applications in the cloud – that's Heroku, utilizing Elixir's scalability and fault tolerance to provide a reliable platform for developers.

Key Learnings:

- Elixir's scalability allows Heroku to handle massive application deployments.
- Fault tolerance ensures platform stability even under high load.

Beyond the Case Studies: Your Elixir Journey Begins

These are just a glimpse into the diverse applications of Elixir. Remember, the possibilities are endless, and the Elixir community is thriving with innovation.

Start Here:

- Explore these popular Elixir frameworks: Phoenix, Ecto, Absinthe.
- Contribute to open-source Elixir projects and learn from the community.
- Build your own applications and experience the power of Elixir firsthand.

By learning from these real-world examples and diving into the Elixir ecosystem, you're equipped to build exceptional applications across industries. Remember, the journey starts with a single step – take yours today and join the growing community of Elixir enthusiasts!

Conclusion

As you conclude your journey through the world of Elixir, remember, this is just the beginning. You've learned the fundamentals, explored powerful tools, and witnessed real-world success stories. Now, it's your turn to unleash the potential of Elixir and craft exceptional applications that stand out.

Embrace the Elixir mindset: Think concurrently, prioritize fault tolerance, and leverage the beauty of functional programming. Remember, Elixir is more than just syntax; it's a philosophy that encourages clean, maintainable, and scalable code.

Join the vibrant community: Elixir boasts a welcoming and supportive community ready to assist you on your journey. Don't hesitate to ask questions, share your creations, and contribute to open-source projects. Learning and giving back go hand-in-hand in this incredible ecosystem.

Start building, experiment, and iterate: The best way to learn is by doing. Don't be afraid to start small, prototype your ideas, and experiment with different approaches. With each iteration, you'll refine your skills and gain invaluable experience.

Remember, the power lies in your hands: Elixir is a powerful tool, but the true magic lies in your vision and creativity. As you embark on your development journey, keep pushing boundaries, explore new possibilities, and build applications that make a difference.

The world of Elixir awaits – step into it with confidence, and start crafting your own story of success!